8ᵗʰ Birthday from Mary Ramsden.
£2

The Young Dragon
Book of Verse

Edited by MICHAEL HARRISON *and*
CHRISTOPHER STUART-CLARK

Oxford University Press

Oxford University Press, Walton Street, Oxford OX2 6DP

Oxford   New York   Toronto
Delhi   Bombay   Calcutta   Madras   Karachi
Petaling Jaya   Singapore   Hong Kong   Tokyo
Nairobi   Dar es Salaam   Cape Town
Melbourne   Auckland

and associated companies in
Berlin   Ibadan

Oxford is a trade mark of Oxford University Press

© Selection and arrangement
Michael Harrison and Christopher Stuart-Clark 1989

First published in this edition 1989

ISBN 0 19 831266 0

Phototypeset by Tradespools Ltd., Frome, Somerset
Printed and bound in Great Britain by
Butler & Tanner Ltd, Frome and London

CONTENTS

THE DOOR OF THE CLASSROOM

Look Out! Max Fatchen	2
Today Jean Little	3
Hill Rolling Andrew Taylor	4
Conkers Clive Sansom	5
Conversation Olive Dove	6
The Quarrel Eleanor Farjeon	7
Cloakroom Barrie Wade	8
Late Judith Nicholls	9
The Description of a Good Boy Henry Dixon	10
Tich Miller Wendy Cope	11
Sally Phoebe Hesketh	12
A Boy's Head Miroslav Holub	13
After English Class Jean Little	14
Drama Lesson Gareth Owen	14
The Nature Lesson Marjorie Baldwin	16
The Blackboard Adrian Mitchell	17
Reuben and Leonard George Crabbe	19
Crystals Barrie Wade	20
Patterns Olive Dehn	22
The Unhappy Schoolboy Anonymous	22
The Dare Judith Nicholls	24
The Climb and the Dream Vernon Scannell	26

WHO ARE YOU?

I'm Nobody, Who are You? Emily Dickinson	30
The Trouble with Geraniums Mervyn Peake	30
A Man of Words Anonymous	31
Truth Barrie Wade	32

A Poison Tree   William Blake   32

Thunderstorms   W. H. Davies   33

Thumbs   Eric Millward   34

My Uncle Paul of Pimlico   Mervyn Peake   35

Johnnie Crack and Flossie Snail   Dylan Thomas   36

Goody Blake and Harry Gill   William Wordsworth   37

Sight   Wilfrid Gibson   40

A Smuggler's Song   Rudyard Kipling   41

Noah   James Reeves   43

Drake's Drum   Sir Henry Newbolt   44

Casabianca   Felicia D. Hemans   45

As He Lay Dying   Randolph Stow   47

Tom Bone   Charles Causley   48

Colours   Frances Evans   49

I COULD TURN AND LIVE WITH ANIMALS

Animals   Walt Whitman   52

The Tiger   Peter Niblett   53

Cage Bird and Sky Bird   Leslie Norris   54

Funeral March   John Fuller   55

How to Catch Tiddlers   Brian Jones   57

The Cat and the Moon   W. B. Yeats   58

Fourteen Ways of Touching the Peter   George MacBeth   59

The Kitten and the Falling Leaves   William Wordsworth   61

Cats and Dogs   Jim Howell   63

Roger the Dog   Ted Hughes   64

Lone Dog   Irene McLeod   65

The Flower-Fed Buffaloes   Vachel Lindsay   66

The Silver Swan   Anonymous   66

Something Told the Wild Geese   Rachel Field   67

The Crow   Russell Hoban   67

Autumn Birds   John Clare   68

The Bee's Last Journey to the Rose   Brian Patten   68

Against Idleness and Mischief   Isaac Watts   69
Squirrels   John Mole   70
Woodlouse   Judith Nicholls   71
After the Rains   N. M. Bodecker   71
Glittering Through the Sky   John Corben   72
Thirteen Blackbirds Look at a Man   R. S. Thomas   73

WHAT STRANGER MIRACLES?

If All the World were Paper   Anonymous   78
Poetry   Eleanor Farjeon   79
Hawthorn White   Charles Causley   79
The Terrible Path   Brian Patten   81
Excelsior   Henry Wadsworth Longfellow   83
The Golden Boy   Ted Hughes   85
Unwelcome   Mary Coleridge   87
The Woman of Water   Adrian Mitchell   88
The Horn   James Reeves   89
The Song of Wandering Aengus   W. B. Yeats   90
Noah's Ark   Roger McGough   91
The North Ship   Philip Larkin   96
Mary Celeste   Judith Nicholls   97
The Sands of Dee   Charles Kingsley   100
Miracles   Walt Whitman   101

WE'LL WEATHER THE WEATHER

Whether   Anonymous   104
The Weather   Gavin Ewart   104
Weathers   Thomas Hardy   105
Summer and Winter   Percy Bysshe Shelley   106
The Pedalling Man   Russell Hoban   107
Rain   Elizabeth Jennings   109

The Mud   Andrew Young   109
The Black Cloud   W. H. Davies   110
Storm   Roger McGough   111
Thunder and Lightning   James Kirkup   111
Ice   Walter de la Mare   112
Snow in the Suburbs   Thomas Hardy   114
Stopping by Woods on a Snowy Evening   Robert Frost   115
The Brook   Alfred, Lord Tennyson   116
Water   Jonathan Kingsman   118
The Hills   Rachel Field   119
Spring Nature Notes   Ted Hughes   120
To Daffodils   Robert Herrick   121
Joys   James Russell Lowell   122
Until I Saw the Sea   Lilian Moore   122
The Sea   R. S. Thomas   123
Old Man Ocean   Russell Hoban   123

WHAT DID I DREAM?

Fear of the Dark   Vernon Scannell   126
Night Clouds   Amy Lowell   127
Is the Moon Tired?   Christina Rossetti   127
Nailsworth Hill   W. H. Davies   128
Quiet   Richard Church   128
Escape at Bedtime   Robert Louis Stevenson   129
Night Walk   Max Fatchen   130
The Lurkers   Adrian Henri   131
Warning to Children   Robert Graves   132
Half Asleep   Gareth Owen   133
To Sleep   William Wordsworth   134
Whatif   Shel Silverstein   135
Travel   Robert Louis Stevenson   136
The Unending Sky   John Masefield   137
What Did I Dream?   Robert Graves   138

Message Understood   Gareth Owen   138

Moon-Wind   Ted Hughes   140

Ballad of the Sad Astronaut   Judith Nicholls   141

Our Solar System   Eric Finney   142

THE DOOR OF THE CLASSROOM

Look Out!

The witches mumble horrid chants,
You're scolded by five thousand aunts,
   A Martian pulls a fearsome face
   And hurls you into Outer Space,
You're tied in front of whistling trains,
A tomahawk has sliced your brains,
   The tigers snarl, the giants roar,
   You're sat on by a dinosaur.
In vain you're shouting 'Help' and 'Stop',
The walls are spinning like a top,
   The earth is melting in the sun
   And all the horror's just begun.
And, oh, the screams, the thumping hearts—
That awful night before school starts.

MAX FATCHEN

Today

Today I will not live up to my potential.
Today I will not relate well to my peer group.
Today I will not contribute in class.
   I will not volunteer one thing.
Today I will not strive to do better.
Today I will not achieve or adjust or grow enriched
   or get involved.
I will not put up my hand even if the teacher is wrong
   and I can prove it.

Today I might eat the eraser off my pencil.
I'll look at clouds.
I'll be late.
I don't think I'll wash.

I need a rest.

JEAN LITTLE

Hill Rolling

I kind of exploded inside,
and joy shot out of me.
I began my roll down the grassy hill.
I bent my knees up small, took a deep breath
and I was off.
My arms shot out sideways.
I gathered speed.
My eyes squinted.
Sky and grass, dazzle and dark.

I went on forever,
My arms were covered with dents,
holes, squashed grass.
Before I knew it I was at the bottom.
The game was over.
The door of the classroom closed behind me.
I can smell chalk dust, and hear the voice of teacher,
to make me forget my hill.

ANDREW TAYLOR

Conkers

When chestnuts are hanging
Above the school yard,
They are little green sea-mines
Spiky and hard.

But when they fall bursting
And all the boys race,
Each shines like a jewel
In a satin case.

CLIVE SANSOM

Conversation

Why are you always tagging on?
You ought to be dressing dolls
Like other sisters.

Dolls! You know I don't like them.
Cold, stiff things lying so still.
Let's go to the woods and climb trees.
The crooked elm is the best.
From the top you can see the river
And the old man hills,
Hump-backed and hungry
As ragged beggars.
In the day they seem small and far away
But at night they crowd closer
And stand like frowning giants.
Come on! What are you waiting for?

I have better things to do.

It's wild in the woods today.
Rooks claw the air with their cackling.

The trees creak and sigh.
They say that long ago, slow Sam the woodcutter
Who liked to sleep in the hollow oak,
Was found dead there.
The sighing is his ghost, crying to come back.
Let's go and hear it.

I hate the sound.

You mean you're afraid?

Of course not.
Jim and I are going fishing.

Can I come too?

What do you know about fishing?
You're only a girl.

OLIVE DOVE

The Quarrel

I quarrelled with my brother
I don't know what about,
One thing led to another
And somehow we fell out.
The start of it was slight,
The end of it was strong,
He said he was right,
I knew he was wrong!

We hated one another.
The afternoon turned black.
Then suddenly my brother
Thumped me on the back,
And said, 'Oh, *come* along!
We can't go on all night—
I was in the wrong.'
So he was in the right.

ELEANOR FARJEON

Cloakroom

Anoraks hang limp and folded,
bats sleeping by day;

when steam rises from racked rows
they are kippers to be smoked.

These pipes are comfort from bullies,
hot and final sanctuary,

and the best place in hide-and-seek
is hanging crucifixed

across two pegs with knees drawn up
beneath a duffle-coat.

I hid once through assembly,
the piano mirage faint

and singing voices lapping
at some distant shore.

My teacher found me drowsed by rain forests
steaming under tropic sun.

She was kind and simply asked
why I was late.

I don't recall my answer, only that
my mind had drained

to rows of empty question-marks
turned upside-down.   BARRIE WADE

Late

You're late, said miss.
The bell has gone,
dinner numbers done
and work begun.

What have you got to say for yourself?

Well, it's like this, miss.
Me mum was sick,
me dad fell down the stairs,
the wheel fell off me bike
and then we lost our Billy's snake
behind the kitchen chairs. Earache
struck down me grampy, me gran
took quite a funny turn.
Then on the way I met this man
whose dog attacked me shin—
look, miss, you can see the blood,
it doesn't look too good,
does it?

Yes, yes, sit down—
and next time say you're sorry
for disturbing all the class.
Now get on with your story,
fast!

Please miss, I've got nothing to write about.

JUDITH NICHOLLS

The Description of a Good Boy

The boy that is good,
Does learn his book well;
And if he can't read,
Will strive for to spell.

His school he does love,
And when he is there,
For play and for toys,
No time can he spare.

His mind is full bent,
On what he is taught;
He sits in the school,
As one full of thought.

Though not as a mope,
Who quakes out of fear
The whip or the rod
Should fall on his rear.

But like a good lad
Who aims to be wise,
He thinks on his book,
And not on his toys.

His mien will be grave,
Yet, if you would know,
He plays with an air,
When a dunce dare not so.

His aim is to learn,
His task is his play;
And when he has learned,
He smiles and looks gay.

HENRY DIXON

Tich Miller

Tich Miller wore glasses
with elastoplast-pink frames
and had one foot three sizes larger than the other.

When they picked teams for outdoor games
she and I were always the last two
left standing by the wire-mesh fence.

We avoided one another's eyes,
stooping, perhaps, to re-tie a shoelace,
or affecting interest in the flight

of some fortunate bird, and pretended
not to hear the urgent conference:
'Have Tubby!' 'No, no, have Tich!'

Usually they chose me, the lesser dud,
and she lolloped, unselected,
to the back of the other team.

At eleven we went to different schools.
In time I learned to get my own back,
sneering at hockey-players who couldn't spell.

Tich died when she was twelve.

WENDY COPE

Sally

She was a dog-rose kind of girl:
elusive, scattery as petals;
scratchy sometimes, tripping you like briars.
She teased the boys
turning this way and that, not to be tamed
or taught any more than the wind.
Even in school the word 'ought'
had no meaning for Sally.
On dull days
she'd sit quiet as a mole at her desk
delving in thought.
But when the sun called
she was gone, running the blue day down
till the warm hedgerows prickled the dusk
and moths flickered out.

Her mother scolded; Dad
gave her the hazel-switch,
said her head was stuffed with feathers
and a starling tongue.
But they couldn't take the shine out of her.
Even when it rained
you felt the sun saved under her skin.
She'd a way of escape
laughing at you from the bright end of a tunnel,
leaving you in the dark.

PHOEBE HESKETH

A Boy's Head

In it there is a space-ship
and a project
for doing away with piano lessons.

And there is
Noah's ark,
which shall be first.

And there is
an entirely new bird,
an entirely new hare,
an entirely new bumble-bee.

There is a river
that flows upwards.

There is a multiplication table.

There is anti-matter.

And it just cannot be trimmed.

I believe
that only what cannot be trimmed
is a head.

There is much promise
in the circumstance
that so many people have heads.

MIROSLAV HOLUB
(Translated by Ian Milner)

After English Class

I used to like 'Stopping by Woods on a Snowy Evening.'
I liked the coming darkness,
The jingle of harness bells, breaking—and adding to
   —the stillness,
the gentle drift of snow . . .

But today, the teacher told us what everything stood for.
The woods, the horse, the miles to go, the sleep—
They all have 'hidden meanings.'

It's grown so complicated now that,
Next time I drive by,
I don't think I'll bother to stop.

JEAN LITTLE

Drama Lesson

'Let's see some super shapes you Blue Group,'
Mr Lavender shouts down the hall.
'And forests don't forget your trembly leaves
And stand up straight and tall.'

But Phillip Chubb is in our group
And he wants to be Robin Hood
And Ann Boot is sulking because she's not with her
friend
And I don't see why I should be wood.

The lights are switched on in the class-rooms,
Outside the sky's nearly black,
And the dining-hall smells of gravy and fat
And Chubb has boils down his back.

Sir tells him straight that he's got to be tree
But he won't wave his arms around.
'How can I wave my branches, Sir,
Friar Tuck has chopped them all down.'

Then I come cantering through Sherwood
To set Maid Marion free
And I really believe I'm Robin Hood
And the Sheriff's my enemy.

At my back my trusty longbow
My broadsword clanks at my side,
My outlaws gallop behind me
As into adventure we ride.

'Untie that maid you villain,' I shout
With all the strength I have,
But the tree has got bored and is picking his nose
And Maid Marion has gone to the lav.

After rehearsals, Sir calls us together
And each group performs their play,
But just as it comes to our turn
The bell goes for the end of the day.

As I trudge my way home through the city streets
The cars and the houses retreat
And a thunder of hooves beats in my mind
And I gallop through acres of wheat.

The castle gleams white in the distance,
The banners flap, golden and red,
And distant trumpets weave silver dreams
In the landscapes of my head.

GARETH OWEN

The Nature Lesson

The teacher has the flowers on her desk,
Then goes round, giving one to each of us.
We are going to study the primrose—
To find out all about it. It has five petals,
Notice the little dent in each, making it heart-shaped
And a pale green calyx (And O! the hairy stem!).
Now, in the middle of the flower
There may be a little knob—that is the pistil—
Or perhaps your flower may show the bunch of stamens.
        We look at our flowers
To find out which kind we have got.

Now we are going to look inside,
So pull your petals off, one by one.
        But wait . . .
If I pull my flower to pieces it will stop
Being a primrose. It will be just bits
Strewn on my desk. I can't pull it to pieces.
What does it matter what goes on inside?
I won't find out by pulling it to pieces,
Because it will not be a primrose any more,
And the bits will not mean anything at all.
A primrose is a primrose, not just bits.

It lies there, a five-petalled primrose,
A whole primrose, a living primrose.
To find out what is inside I make it dead,
And then it will not be a primrose.
        You can't find out
What goes on inside a living flower that way.
The teacher talks, fingers rustle . . .

I will look over my neighbour's flower
And leave my primrose whole. But if the teacher comes
And tells me singly to pull my flower to pieces
Then I will do as I am told. The teacher comes,
Passes my neighbour on her gangway side,
Does not see my primrose is still whole,
Goes by, not noticing, nobody notices.

My flower remains a primrose, that they all
Want to find out about by pulling to pieces.
I am alone: all the world is alone
In the flower left breathing on my desk.

MARJORIE BALDWIN

The Blackboard

Five foot by five foot
(The smalls have measured it).
Smooth black surface
(Wiped by a small after every class).
Five different colours of chalk
And a class of twenty-five smalls,
One big.

Does the big break up the chalk
Into twenty-five or twenty-six
And invite the smalls to make
A firework show of colours
Shapes and words
Starting on the blackboard

But soon overflowing
  All over the room
  All over the school
  All over the town
  All over the country
  All over the world?

  No.

The big looks at the textbook
Which was written by a big
And published by a firm of bigs.
The textbook says
The names and dates of Nelson's battles.
So the big writes, in white,
Upon the black of the blackboard,
The names and dates of Nelson's battles.
The smalls copy into their books
The names and dates of Nelson's battles.

  Nelson was a big
Who died fighting for freedom or something.

ADRIAN MITCHELL

Reuben and Leonard

Poor *Reuben Dixon* has the noisiest school
Of ragged lads, who ever bow'd to rule;
Low in his price—the men who heave our coals
And clean our causeways, send him boys in shoals;
To see poor Reuben, with his fry beside,—
Their half-check'd rudeness, and his half-scorned pride,—
Their room, the sty in which th' assembly meet,
In the close lane behind the Northgate street;
T'observe his vain attempts to keep the peace,
Till tolls the bell, and strife and troubles cease,—
Calls for our praise; his labour praise deserves,
But not our pity; Reuben has no nerves:
'Mid noise and dirt, and stench, and play, and prate,
He calmly cuts the pen or views the slate.

But *Leonard*!—yes, for Leonard's fate I grieve,
Who loathes the station which he dares not leave:
He cannot dig, he will not beg his bread,
All his dependence rests upon his head;
And deeply skill'd in sciences and arts,
On vulgar lads he wastes superior parts.

Alas! what grief that feeling mind sustains,
In guiding hands, and stirring torpid brains;
He whose proud mind from pole to pole will move,
And view the wonders of the worlds above;
Who thinks and reasons strongly:—hard his fate,
Confined for ever to the pen and slate:
True, he submits, and when the long dull day
Has slowly passed, in weary tasks away,
To other worlds with cheerful view he looks
And parts the night between repose and books.

Amid his labours, he has sometimes tried
To turn a little from his cares aside;
Pope, Milton, Dryden, with delight has seized,
His soul engaged, and of his trouble eased;
When, with a heavy eye and ill-done sum,
No part conceived, a stupid boy will come;
Then Leonard first subdues the rising frown,
And bids the blockhead lay his blunders down;
O'er which disgusted he will turn his eye;
To his sad duty his sound mind apply,
And, vex'd in spirit, throw his pleasures by.

GEORGE CRABBE

Crystals

First, in saucers we spread salt.
Our imagination turns

its shimmer into spoil heaps
drawn from far-off diamond mines

beneath the tawny plain
of Africa. We hold this dream

until the drench of water
vanquishes their fire.

A string of disappearing pools,
we range them along windowsills

and the sun steals in on lion's paws
to lap away their drink.

Our teacher mixes 'poison'
in a glass apart for safety;

it attracts us like a blinding sky
of fierce, ice-shattering blue.

Our waterholes days later
have dried up to brittle crusts

of sharp-edged crystals
glittering like splintered glass.

Ice-wonder fills our eyes
almost to snow-blinding.

Our teacher's soft brown palm
shows diamonds of blue

deeper than sky or sea.
Her eyes sparkle ice and fire.

BARRIE WADE

Patterns

The other side of learning is forgetting.
How can you open your eyes if they don't close?
Teachers find this very upsetting.
They like you to be always on your toes.

Anybody can see that x equals y
When it's written in white chalk on a black wall,
Just as anyone can see that a black cloud in a blue sky
Means that rain is going to fall.

Tidy children are good, untidy children are slatterns.
Everything is labelled according to looks.
But beneath our lids spring rainbow-coloured patterns
That were never found in books.

OLIVE DEHN

The Unhappy Schoolboy

HEY! hey! by this day!
What availeth it me though I say nay?

I would fain be a clerk,
But yet it is a strange work;
The birchen twigs be so sharp,
It maketh me have a faint heart.
What availeth it me though I say nay?

On Monday in the morning when I shall rise
At six of the clock, it is the guise
To go to school without advice—
I would rather go twenty miles twice!
　　What availeth it me though I say nay?

My master looketh as he were mad:
'Where hast thou been, thou sorry lad?'
'Milking ducks, as my mother bade':
It was no marvel that I were sad.
　　What availeth it me though I say nay?

My master peppered my tail with good speed,
It was worse than fennel seed,
He would not leave till it did bleed.
Much sorrow have he for his deed!
　　What availeth it me though I say nay?

I would my master were a hare,
And all his books greyhounds were,
And I myself a jolly hunter;
To blow my horn I would not spare,
For if he were dead I would not care!
　　What availeth it me though I say nay?

ANONYMOUS

The Dare

Go on, I dare you,
come on down!

Was it *me* they called?
Pretend you haven't heard,
a voice commanded in my mind.
Walk past, walk fast
and don't look down,
don't look behind.

Come on, it's easy!

The banks were steep,
the water low
and flanked with oozing brown.
Easy? Walk fast
but don't look down.
Walk straight, walk on,
even risk their jeers
and run . . .

Never go near those dykes,
my mother said.
No need to tell me.
I'd seen stones sucked in
and covered without trace,
gulls slide to bobbing safety,
grasses drown as water rose.
No need to tell me
to avoid the place.

She ca-a-a-n't, she ca-a-a-n't!
Cowardy, cowardy custard!

There's no such word as 'can't',
my father said.
I slowed my pace.
The voices stopped,
waited as I wavered, grasping breath.
My mother's wrath? My father's scorn?
A water death?

I hesitated then turned back,
forced myself to see the mud below.
After all, it was a dare . . .
There was no choice;
I had to go.

JUDITH NICHOLLS

The Climb and the Dream

The boy had never seen the tree before;
He thought it was a splendid one to climb,
The branches strong enough to take far more
Than his slight weight; and, while they did not rhyme
In perfect echoes of each other's shape,
They were arranged in useful patterns which
He found as thrilling as a fire-escape.
Now was his chance! He hopped across the ditch
And wriggled underneath the rusty wire,
And then he found himself confronted by
The lofty challenge, suddenly much higher
Now he was at its foot. He saw the sky
Through foliage and branches, broken like
A pale blue china plate. He leapt and clung
To the lowest branch and swung from left to right.
Then heaved himself astride the swaying rung.
With cautious hands and feet he made a start
From branch to branch; dust tickled in his throat.
He smelt the dark green scent of leaf and bark;
Malicious thorny fingers clutched his coat
And once clawed at his forehead, drawing blood.
Sweat drenched his aching body, blurred his eyes,
But he climbed up and up until he stood
Proud on the highest bough and, with surprise,
Looked down to see the shrunken fields and streams
As if his climb had re-created them;
And he was sure that, often, future dreams
Would bring this vision back to him. But then
A sudden darkening came upon the sky,
He felt the breeze grow burlier and chill,
Joy drained away. And then he realized why:
This was a tree he'd scaled, and not a hill—

The journey down would not be easier
But much more difficult than his ascent:
The foothold surfaces seemed greasier
And less accessible, and he had spent
Much of strength, was very close to tears,
And sick with fear, yet knew he must go down.
The thing he dreamt about in after-years
Was not the moment when he wore the crown
Of gold achievement in the highest bough
Above the common world of strife and pain,
But the ordeal of dark descent, and how
He sobbed with joy to reach safe earth again.

VERNON SCANNELL

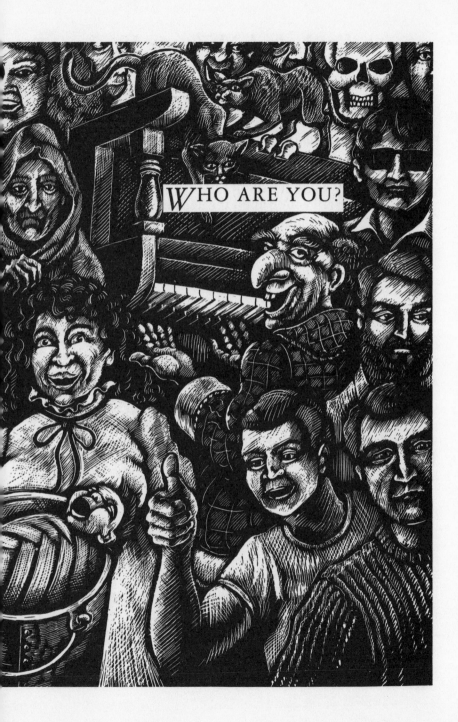

I'm Nobody! Who are You?

I'm Nobody! Who are you?
Are you – Nobody – Too?
Then there's a pair of us!
Don't tell! They'd banish us you know!

How dreary – to be – Somebody!
How public – like a Frog –
To tell your name – the livelong June –
To an admiring Bog!

EMILY DICKINSON

The Trouble with Geraniums

The trouble with geraniums
is that they're much too red!
The trouble with my toast is that
it's far too full of bread.

The trouble with a diamond
is that it's much too bright.
The same applies to fish and stars
and the electric light.

The trouble with the stars I see
lies in the way they fly.
The trouble with myself is all
self-centred in the eye.

The trouble with my looking-glass
is that it shows me, me:
there's trouble in all sorts of things
where it should never be.

MERVYN PEAKE

A Man of Words

A man of words and not of deeds
Is like a garden full of weeds;
And when the weeds begin to grow,
It's like a garden full of snow;
And when the snow begins to fall,
It's like a bird upon the wall;
And when the bird away does fly,
It's like an eagle in the sky;
And when the sky begins to roar,
It's like a lion at the door;
And when the door begins to crack,
It's like a stick across your back;
And when your back begins to smart,
It's like a penknife in your heart;
And when your heart begins to bleed,
You're dead, and dead, and dead indeed.

ANONYMOUS

Truth

Sticks and stones may break my bones,
but words can also hurt me.
Stones and sticks break only skin,
while words are ghosts that haunt me.

Slant and curved the word-swords fall
to pierce and stick inside me.
Bats and bricks may ache through bones,
but words can mortify me.

Pain from words has left its scar
on mind and heart that's tender.
Cuts and bruises now have healed;
it's words that I remember.

BARRIE WADE

A Poison Tree

I was angry with my friend:
I told my wrath, my wrath did end.
I was angry with my foe:
I told it not, my wrath did grow.

And I watered it in fears,
Night and morning with my tears;
And I sunned it with smiles,
And with soft deceitful wiles.

And it grew both day and night,
Till it bore an apple bright;
And my foe beheld it shine,
And he knew that it was mine,

And into my garden stole
When the night had veiled the pole:
In the morning glad I see
My foe outstretched beneath the tree.

WILLIAM BLAKE

Thunderstorms

My mind has thunderstorms,
    That brood for heavy hours:
Until they rain me words,
    My thoughts are drooping flowers
And sulking, silent birds.

Yet come, dark thunderstorms,
    And brood your heavy hours;
For when you rain me words,
    My thoughts are dancing flowers
And joyful singing birds.

W. H. DAVIES

Thumbs

A thumb is half a pinch,
a fifth of a fist;

is for keeping things
under, helps hold a pint.

It gives its name
to arbitrary rules;

its nail can catch a
character, gouge eyes.

Tyrants' thumbs granted
pardon or dispatch.

Incalculable is the
power of thumbs:

forget your thumbs for a day,
try being all fingers.

Without your thumbs you've
got a fight on your hands.

ERIC MILLWARD

My Uncle Paul of Pimlico

My Uncle Paul of Pimlico
Has seven cats as white as snow,
Who sit at his enormous feet
And watch him, as a special treat,
Play the piano upside-down,
In his delightful dressing-gown;
The firelight leaps, the parlour glows,
And, while the music ebbs and flows,
They smile (while purring the refrains),
At little thoughts that cross their brains.

MERVYN PEAKE

Johnnie Crack and Flossie Snail

Johnnie Crack and Flossie Snail
Kept their baby in a milking pail
Flossie Snail and Johnnie Crack
One would pull it out and one would put it back

O it's my turn now said Flossie Snail
To take the baby from the milking pail
And it's my turn now said Johnnie Crack
To smack it on the head and put it back

Johnnie Crack and Flossie Snail
Kept their baby in a milking pail
One would put it back and one would pull it out
And all it had to drink was ale and stout
For Johnnie Crack and Flossie Snail
Always used to say that stout and ale
Was *good* for a baby in a milking pail.

DYLAN THOMAS

Goody Blake and Harry Gill
A True Story

Oh! what's the matter? what's the matter?
What is't that ails young Harry Gill?
That evermore his teeth they chatter,
Chatter, chatter, chatter still!
At night, at morning, and at noon,
'Tis all the same with Harry Gill;
Beneath the sun, beneath the moon,
His teeth they chatter, chatter still!

Young Harry was a lusty drover,
And who so stout of limb as he?
His cheeks were red as ruddy clover;
His voice was like the voice of three.
Old Goody Blake was old and poor;
Ill fed she was, and thinly clad;
And any man who passed her door
Might see how poor a hut she had.

Remote from sheltered village-green,
On a hill's northern side she dwelt,
Where from sea-blasts the hawthorns lean,
And hoary dews are slow to melt.
'Twas well enough, when summer came,
The long, warm, lightsome summer day,
Then at her door the canty Dame
Would sit, as any linnet, gay.

But when the ice our streams did fetter,
Oh then how her old bones would shake!
You would have said, if you had met her,
'Twas a hard time for Goody Blake.
Her evenings then were dull and dead:
Sad case it was, as you may think,
For very cold to go to bed;
And then for cold not sleep a wink.

Now, when the frost was past enduring,
And made her poor old bones to ache,
Could anything be more alluring
Than the old hedge to Goody Blake?
And now and then, it must be said,
When her old bones were cold and chill,
She left her fire or left her bed,
To seek the hedge of Harry Gill.

Now Harry he had long suspected
This trespass of old Goody Blake;
And vowed that she should be detected –
That he on her would vengeance take.
And oft from his warm fire he'd go,
And to the fields his road would take,
And there, at night, in frost and snow,
He watch'd to seize old Goody Blake.

And once, behind a rick of barley,
Thus looking out did Harry stand:
The moon was full and shining clearly,
And crisp with frost the stubble land.
– He hears a noise – he's all awake –
Again? – on tip-toe down the hill
He softly creeps – 'tis Goody Blake;
She's at the hedge of Harry Gill!

Right glad was he when he beheld her:
Stick after stick did Goody pull,
He stood behind a bush of elder,
Till she had filled her apron full.
When with her load she turned about,
The by-way back again to take;
He started forward, with a shout,
And sprang upon poor Goody Blake.

And fiercely by the arm he took her,
And by the arm he held her fast,
And fiercely by the arm he shook her,
And cried, 'I've caught you then at last!'
Then Goody, who had nothing said,
Her bundle from her lap let fall;
And kneeling on the sticks, she prayed
To God that is the judge of all.

She prayed, her withered hand uprearing,
While Harry held her by the arm –
'God! who are never out of hearing,
O may he never more be warm!'
The cold, cold moon above her head,
Thus on her knees did Goody pray;
Young Harry heard what she had said:
And icy cold he turned away.

He went complaining all the morrow
That he was cold and very chill:
His face was gloom, his heart was sorrow,
Alas! that day for Harry Gill!
And Harry's flesh it fell away;
And all who see him say, 'tis plain,
That, live as long as live he may,
He never will be warm again.

No word to any man he utters,
A-bed or up, to young or old;
But ever to himself he mutters,
'Poor Harry Gill is very cold.'
A-bed or up, by night or day;
His teeth they chatter, chatter still.
Now think, ye farmers all, I pray,
Of Goody Blake and Harry Gill!

WILLIAM WORDSWORTH

Sight

By the lamplight stall I loitered, feasting my eyes
On colours ripe and rich for the heart's desire –
Tomatoes redder than Krakatoa's fire,
Oranges like old sunsets over Tyre,
And apples golden-green as the glades of Paradise.

And as I lingered lost in divine delight,
My heart thanked God for the goodly gift of sight

· · · · ·

When suddenly behind me in the night
I heard the tapping of a blind man's stick.

WILFRID GIBSON

A Smuggler's Song

If you wake at midnight, and hear a horse's feet,
Don't go drawing back the blind, or looking in the street,
Them that ask no questions isn't told a lie.
Watch the wall, my darling, while the Gentlemen go by!
      Five and twenty ponies,
      Trotting through the dark—
      Brandy for the Parson,
      'Baccy for the Clerk;
      Laces for a lady, letters for a spy,
And watch the wall, my darling, while the Gentlemen go by!

Running round the woodlump if you chance to find
Little barrels, roped and tarred, all full of brandy-wine,
Don't you shout to come and look, nor use 'em for your play.
Put the brushwood back again—and they'll be gone next day!

If you see the stable-door setting open wide;
If you see a tired horse lying down inside;
If your mother mends a coat cut about and tore;
If the lining's wet and warm—don't you ask no more!

If you meet King George's men, dressed in blue and red,
You be careful what you say, and mindful what is said.
If they call you 'pretty maid', and chuck you 'neath the chin,
Don't you tell where no one is, nor yet where no one's been!

Knocks and footsteps round the house—whistles after dark—
You've no call for running out till the house-dogs bark.
Trusty's here, and *Pincher's* here, and see how dumb they lie—
They don't fret to follow when the Gentlemen go by!

If you do as you've been told, 'likely there's a chance,
You'll be give a dainty doll, all the way from France,
With a cap of Valenciennes, and a velvet hood—
A present from the Gentlemen, along o' being good!
    Five and twenty ponies,
    Trotting through the dark—
    Brandy for the Parson,
    'Baccy for the Clerk.
Them that ask no questions isn't told a lie—
Watch the wall, my darling, while the Gentlemen go by!

RUDYARD KIPLING

Noah

Noah was an Admiral;
Never a one but he
Sailed for forty days and nights
With wife and children three
On such a mighty sea.

Under his tempest-battered deck
This Admiral had a zoo;
And all the creatures in the world,
He kept them, two by two—
Ant, hippo, kangaroo,

And every other beast beside,
Of every mould and make.
When tempests howled and thunder growled
How they did cower and quake
To feel the vessel shake!

But Noah was a Carpenter
Had made his ship so sound
That not a soul of crew or zoo
In all that time was drowned
Before they reached dry ground.

So Admiral, Keeper, Carpenter—
Now should *you* put to sea
In such a flood, it would be good
If one of these you be,
But better still—all three!

JAMES REEVES

Drake's Drum

Drake he's in his hammock an' a thousand miles away,
  (Capten, art tha sleepin' there below?),
Slung atween the round shot in Nombre Dios Bay,
  An' dreamin' arl the time o' Plymouth Hoe.
Yarnder lumes the Island, yarnder lie the ships,
  Wi' sailor lads a dancin' heel-an'-toe,
An' the shore-lights flashin', an' the night-tide dashin',
  He sees et arl so plainly as he saw et long ago.

Drake he was a Devon man, an' rüled the Devon seas,
  (Capten, art tha sleepin' there below?),
Rovin' tho' his death fell, he went wi' heart at ease,
  An' dreamin' arl the time o' Plymouth Hoe.
'Take my drum to England, hang et by the shore,
  Strike et when your powder's runnin' low;
If the Dons sight Devon, I'll quit the port o' Heaven,
  An' drum them up the Channel as we drummed them long
    ago.'

Drake he's in his hammock till the great Armadas come,
  (Capten, art tha sleepin' there below?),
Slung atween the round shot, listenin' for the drum,
  An' dreamin' arl the time o' Plymouth Hoe.
Call him on the deep sea, call him up the Sound,
  Call him when ye sail to meet the foe;
Where the old trade's plyin' an' the old flag flyin'
  They shall find him ware an' wakin', as they found him
    long ago!

SIR HENRY NEWBOLT

Casabianca

The boy stood on the burning deck,
    Whence all but he had fled;
The flame that lit the battle's wreck
    Shone round him o'er the dead.

Yet beautiful and bright he stood,
    As born to rule the storm;
A creature of heroic blood,
    A proud though childlike form.

The flames rolled on; he would not go
    Without his father's word;
That father, faint in death below,
    His voice no longer heard.

He called aloud, 'Say, Father, say,
    If yet my task be done!'
He knew not that the chieftain lay
    Unconscious of his son.

'Speak, Father!' once again he cried,
    'If I may yet be gone!'
And but the booming shots replied,
    And fast the flames rolled on.

Upon his brow he felt their breath,
    And in his waving hair,
And looked from that lone post of death
    In still yet brave despair;

And shouted but once more aloud,
  'My Father! must I stay?'
While o'er him fast, through sail and shroud,
  The wreathing fires made way.

They wrapped the ship in splendour wild,
  They caught the flag on high,
And streamed above the gallant child,
  Like banners in the sky.

There came a burst of thunder sound;
  The boy—Oh! where was he?
Ask of the winds, that far around
  With fragments strewed the sea—

With mast and helm and pennon fair,
  That well had borne their part—
But the noblest thing that perished there
  Was that young, faithful heart.

FELICIA D. HEMANS

As He Lay Dying

As he lay dying, two fat crows
  Sat perched above in a strangling vine,
    And one crow called to the other:
      'Brother,
Harvest his eyes, his tongue is mine.'

As he lay dying, two lithe hawks
  Caressed the wind and spied two crows;
    And one hawk hissed to the other:
      'Brother,
Mine is the sleekest one of those.'

As he lay dying, two eagles passed
  And saw two hawks that hung in flying,
    And one said soft to the other:
      'Brother,
Mark your prey.' As he lay dying.

RANDOLPH STOW

Tom Bone

My name is Tom Bone,
I live all alone
In a deep house on Winter Street.
   Through my mud wall
   The wolf-spiders crawl
   And the mole has his beat.

On my roof of green grass
All the day footsteps pass
In the heat and the cold,
   As snug in a bed
   With my name at its head
   One great secret I hold.

Tom Bone, when the owls rise
In the drifting night skies
Do you walk round about?
   All the solemn hours through
   I lie down just like you
   And sleep the night out.

Tom Bone, as you lie there
On your pillow of hair,
What grave thoughts do you keep?
   Tom says, 'Nonsense and stuff!
   You'll know soon enough.
   Sleep, darling, sleep.'

CHARLES CAUSLEY

Colours

Red is death, for people who are dying,
Silver is tears, for people who are crying,
Blue is a pool, cool and still,
Green is a beautiful grassy hill.

Grey is for people in the early evening,
Black is a dress for people grieving,
Brown is for an old queen's gown,
Gold for a princess's crown.

FRANCES EVANS

I COULD TURN AND LIVE WITH ANIMALS

Animals

I think I could turn and live with animals, they are
　　so placid and self-contained;
I stand and look at them long and long.

They do not sweat and whine about their condition;
They do not lie awake in the dark and weep for
　　their sins;

They do not make me sick discussing their duty to
　　God;
Not one is dissatisfied—not one is demented with the
　　mania of owning things;

Not one kneels to another, nor to his kind that lived
　　thousands of years ago;
Not one is respectable or industrious over the whole
　　earth.

WALT WHITMAN

The Tiger

The tiger behind the bars of his cage growls,
The tiger behind the bars of his cage snarls,
The tiger behind the bars of his cage roars.

Then he thinks.

It would be nice not to be behind bars all
The time
Because they spoil my view
I wish I were wild, not on show.
But if I were wild, hunters might shoot me,
But if I were wild, food might poison me,
But if I were wild, water might drown me.

Then he stops thinking

And . . .

The tiger behind the bars of his cage growls,
The tiger behind the bars of his cage snarls,
The tiger behind the bars of his cage roars.

PETER NIBLETT

Cage Bird and Sky Bird

Cage Bird swung
From an apple tree
And his cage was of silver
And ivory.
  Nobody can be so happy, so happy;
    Sang the Cage Bird.

Sky Bird sang
From a cloudless sky
And his wings were wide
And bright his eye.
  Nobody can be as happy as I;
    Sang the Sky Bird.

That wild song
To the garden fell
And Cage Bird heard it, in
His silver cell.
  Are you free then, are you truly free?
    Cried the Cage Bird.

Sky Bird flew
In the trail of the sun
And swiftly he soared, away
From the garden.
  Sadly sang Cage Bird, when the day was done;
    Sang the Cage Bird.

LESLIE NORRIS

Funeral March

Here come the hounds alive from the kennels.
Keen for their taste of Mr Reynolds.

Here comes the Master with set lips.
Here comes the Huntsman. Here come the Whips.

Here comes the Hunt in black and red.
Colour of death and colour of blood.

The Hunt is after you. Beware!
O Mr Reynolds, take care, take care!

A cup is raised in the village square.
A bell rings roundly through the air.

How quiet the meadows, like a sea
Shifting the wrecks of woods so silently!

The bell rings out and rings its fill
And all the little farms are still.

The Hunt is setting off. Beware!
O Mr Reynolds, take care, take care!

Past the church and through a gate
Trots in line the fox's fate.

The cautious Huntsman slows and stops.
The hounds are worrying a nearby copse.

O Mr Reynolds, were you there?
And left your odour on the air?

The eager hounds from nose to tail
Quiver as they sniff your trail.

They lift their ears, and growl and whine.
Then openly they own the line.

Hear the horn and holloas sing!
Hear the pack's wild yelping ring!

Hear the smallest rider's shout:
Oh they will surely find you out!

The hounds are busy and intent,
Now feathering to chase the scent.

Now the Huntsman's viewed his quarry.
Danger, Mr Reynolds, hurry!

There, there beyond the stream—
A brush of russet tipped with cream.

Now disappearing in the trees,
Padding softly at his ease.

The Hunt is after you. Beware!
O Mr Reynolds, take care, take care!

JOHN FULLER

How to Catch Tiddlers

Watch the net drift. Grey tides
Mingle what purposes your eye supposed
But watch the net. There is no fish
Only the net, the way it moves. There is no fish,
Forget the fish. The net is spread
And moving. Steer gently. Keep the hand
Pressured constantly against the stream.
There is no catch now, only the net
And your pressure and your poise. Below
Ignore the pebbles and the promising weed
Mooning over its secrets. There is just the net,
The hand, and, now, near an old glance
        somewhere
A sleek shape holding its body constant,
Firm in its fluid world. Move on. Watch
Only the net. You are a hand only,
Steering, controlling. Now look.
Inside that silent bulge the shape
Breaks black and firm. You may rise,
You may rise now—the deftest
Turn of the wrist will do it. Your hand
Crude again can support the cling of mesh.
You can relax, coldly note
The titchy black squirm. You have achieved.
Commit success to jamjars. Lean again.
Dip the slack net. Let it belly.

BRIAN JONES

The Cat and the Moon

The cat went here and there
And the moon spun round like a top,
And the nearest kin of the moon,
The creeping cat, looked up.
Black Minnaloushe stared at the moon,
For, wander and wail as he would,
The pure cold light in the sky
Troubled his animal blood.
Minnaloushe runs in the grass
Lifting his delicate feet.
Do you dance, Minnaloushe, do you dance?
When two close kindred meet,
What better than call a dance?
Maybe the moon may learn,
Tired of that courtly fashion,
A new dance turn.
Minnaloushe creeps through the grass
From moonlit place to place,
The sacred moon overhead
Has taken a new phase.
Does Minnaloushe know that his pupils
Will pass from change to change,
And that from round to crescent,
From crescent to round they range?
Minnaloushe creeps through the grass
Alone, important and wise,
And lifts to the changing moon
His changing eyes.

W. B. YEATS

Fourteen Ways of Touching the Peter

I You can push
your thumb
in the
ridge
between his
shoulder-blades
to please him.

II Starting
at its root,
you can let
his whole
tail
flow
through your hand.

III Forming
a fist
you can let
him rub
his bone
skull
against it, hard.

IV When he makes
bread,
you can lift
him
by his under-
sides on your
knuckles.

V In hot
weather
you can itch
the fur
under
his chin. He
likes that.

VI At night
you can hoist
him
out of his bean-stalk,
sleepily
clutching
paper bags.

VII Pressing
his head against
your cheek,
you can carry
him
in the dark,
safely.

VIII In late Autumn
you can find
seeds
adhering
to his fur.
There are
plenty.

59

IX You can prise
    his jaws
    open,
    helping
    any medicine
    he won't
    abide, go down.

X   You can touch
    his
    feet, only
    if
    he is relaxed.
    He
    doesn't like it.

XI You can comb
    spare thin
    fur
    from his coat,
    so he won't
    get
    fur ball.

XII You can shake
     his rigid
     chicken-leg leg,
     scouring his
     hind-quarters
     with his Vim
     tongue.

XIII Dumping
      hot fish
      on his plate, you can
      fend
      him off,
      pushing
      and purring.

XIV You can have
     him shrimp
     along you,
     breathing,
     whenever
     you want
     to compose poems.

GEORGE MACBETH

The Kitten and the Falling Leaves

See the kitten on the wall,
Sporting with the leaves that fall,
Withered leaves—one, two, and three—
From the lofty elder-tree!
Through the calm and frosty air
Of this morning bright and fair,
Eddying round and round they sink
Softly, slowly; one might think
From the motions that are made,
Every little leaf conveyed
Sylph or faery hither tending,
To his lower world descending,
Each invisible and mute,
In his wavering parachute.

But the kitten, how she starts,
Crouches, stretches paws, and darts!
First at one, and then its fellow
Just as light and just as yellow.
There are many now—now one—
Now they stop and there are none.

What intenseness of desire
In her upward eye of fire!
With a tiger-leap half way
Now she meets the coming prey,
Lets it go as fast, and then
Has it in her power again:
Now she works with three or four,
Like an Indian conjuror;
Quick as he in feats of art,
Far beyond in joy of heart.
Were her antics played in the eye
Of a thousand standers-by,
Clapping hands with shout and stare,
What would little Tabby care
For the plaudits of the crowd?

WILLIAM WORDSWORTH

Cats

have eyes that yawn,
green
as a halt sign.

In morse-tail
language
they speak your mind,

loving you
to fur-deep
distraction.

Dogs

eat gratefully,
relish the tongue's spit,
jowl-smack;

ear-flip
at sleep's tale
of old carpets;

hold faith
in the warm here
of hands;

wagging

move in dreams
to the world's
lollop.

JIM HOWELL

Roger the Dog

Asleep he wheezes at his ease.
He only wakes to scratch his fleas.

He hogs the fire, he bakes his head
As if it were a loaf of bread.

He's just a sack of snoring dog.
You can lug him like a log.

You can roll him with your foot,
He'll stay snoring where he's put.

I take him out for exercise,
He rolls in cowclap up to his eyes.

He will not race, he will not romp,
He saves his strength for gobble and chomp.

He'll work as hard as you could wish
Emptying his dinner dish,

Then flops flat, and digs down deep,
Like a miner, into sleep.

TED HUGHES

Lone Dog

I'm a lean dog, a keen dog, a wild dog and lone,
I'm a rough dog, a tough dog, hunting on my own!
I'm a bad dog, a mad dog, teasing silly sheep;
I love to sit and bay at the moon and keep fat souls from sleep.

I'll never be a lap dog, licking dirty feet,
A sleek dog, a meek dog, cringing for my meat.
Not for me the fireside, the well-filled plate,
But shut the door and sharp stone and cuff and kick and hate.

Not for me the other dogs, running by my side,
Some have run a short while, but none of them would bide.
O mine is still the lone trail, the hard trail, the best,
Wide wind and wild stars and the hunger of the quest.

IRENE McLEOD

65

The Flower-Fed Buffaloes

The flower-fed buffaloes of the spring
In the days of long ago,
Ranged where the locomotives sing
And the prairie flowers lie low: –
The tossing, blooming, perfumed grass
Is swept away by the wheat,
Wheels and wheels and wheels spin by
In the spring that still is sweet.
But the flower-fed buffaloes of the spring
Left us, long ago.
They gore no more, they bellow no more
They trundle around the hills no more: –
With the Blackfeet, lying low,
With the Pawnees, lying low,
Lying low.

VACHEL LINDSAY

The Silver Swan

The silver swan, who living had no note,
When death approached, unlocked her silent throat,
Leaning her breast against the reedy shore,
Thus sung her first and last, and sung no more:
'Farewell all joys! O death, come close mine eyes;
More geese than swans now live, more fools than wise.'

ANONYMOUS

Something Told the Wild Geese

Something told the wild geese
    It was time to go,
Though the fields lay golden
    Something whispered, 'Snow!'
Leaves were green and stirring,
    Berries, luster-glossed,
But beneath warm feathers
    Something cautioned, 'Frost!'

All the sagging orchards
    Steamed with amber spice,
But each wild breast stiffened
    At remembered ice.
Something told the wild geese
    It was time to fly—
Summer sun was on their wings,
    Winter in their cry.

RACHEL FIELD

The Crow

Flying loose and easy, where does he go
Swaggering in the sky, what does he know,
Why is he laughing, the carrion crow?
Why is he shouting, why won't he sing,
How did he steal them, whom will he bring
Loaves of blue heaven under each wing?

RUSSELL HOBAN

Autumn Birds

The wild duck startles like a sudden thought,
And heron slow as if it might be caught;
The flopping crows on weary wing go by,
And greybeard jackdaws, noising as they fly;
The crowds of starlings whizz and hurry by
And darken like a cloud the evening sky;
The larks like thunder rise and suther round
Then drop and nest in the stubble ground;
The wild swan hurries high and noises loud,
With white necks peering to the evening cloud.
The weary rooks to distant woods are gone;
With length of tail the magpie winnows on
To neighbouring tree, and leaves the distant crow,
While small birds nestle in the hedge below.

JOHN CLARE

The Bee's Last Journey to the Rose

I came first through the warm grass
Humming with spring,
And now swim through the evening's
Soft sunlight gone cold.
I'm old in this green ocean,
Going a final time to the rose.

North Wind, until I reach it,
Keep your icy breath away
That changes pollen into dust.
Let me be drunk on this scent a final time.
Then blow if you must.

BRIAN PATTEN

Against Idleness and Mischief

How doth the little busy bee
  Improve each shining hour,
And gather honey all the day
  From every opening flower!

How skilfully she builds her cell!
  How neat she spreads the wax!
And labours hard to store it well
  With the sweet food she makes.

In works of labour or of skill
  I would be busy too:
For Satan finds some mischief still
  For idle hands to do.

In books, or work, or healthful play.
  Let my first years be past,
That I may give for every day
  Some good account at last.

ISAAC WATTS

Squirrels

Tails like dandelion clocks
They blow away, these
Light-weight bucking broncos
With a plume behind.

For sheer surprise
No well-aimed burdock
Sticks more nimbly to your overcoat
Than these to tree bark,

Nor with such aplomb
Can any comparable creature
Lead a dance more deftly
Through the branches.

Down to earth again, they
Hold their tums in, little aldermen,
Or sit on tree stumps
Like old ladies knitting socks.

JOHN MOLE

Woodlouse

Armoured dinosaur,
blundering through jungle grass by
dandelion-light.

Knight's headpiece, steel-hinged
orange-segment, ball-bearing,
armadillo-drop.

Pale peppercorn, pearled
eyeball; sentence without end,
my rolling full-stop.

JUDITH NICHOLLS

After the Rains

After the rains,
when I opened my door
the spiders were at it
as hard as before,

mending their nets,
as the sun came again,
the patient, dependable
fly-fishermen.

N. M. BODECKER

Glittering Through the Sky

Glittering through the sky
Insects land safely
At scarlet supermarkets,
The shelves stacked with nectar.

My food flies off.
I cannot soar after
But must scuttle through
The dead leaves.

Out of my abdomen
I spin sticky ropes—
Fill the green freeways
With my shopping trolley.

JOHN CORBEN

Thirteen Blackbirds
Look at a Man

1

It is calm.
It is as though
we lived in a garden
that had not yet arrived
at the knowledge of
good and evil.
But there is a man in it.

2

There will be
rain falling vertically
from an indifferent
sky. There will stare out
from behind its
bars the face of the man
who is not enjoying it.

3

Nothing higher
than a blackberry
bush. As the sun comes up
fresh, what is the darkness
stretching from horizon
to horizon? It is the shadow
here of the forked man.

4

We have eaten
the blackberries and spat out
the seeds, but they lie
glittering like the eyes of a man.

5

After we have stopped
singing, the garden is disturbed
by echoes; it is
the man whistling, expecting
everything to come to him.

6

We wipe our beaks
on the branches
wasting the dawn's
jewellery to get rid
of the taste of a man.

7

Nevertheless,
which is not the case
with a man, our
bills give us no trouble.

8

Who said the
number was unlucky?
It was the man, who,
trying to pass us,
had his licence endorsed
thirteen times.

9

In the cool
of the day the garden
seems given over
to blackbirds. Yet
we know also that somewhere
there is a man in hiding.

10

To us there are
eggs and there are
blackbirds. But there is the man,
too, trying without feathers
to incubate a solution.

11

We spread our
wings, reticulating
our air-space. A man stands
under us and worries
at his ability to do the same.

12

When night comes
like a visitor
from outer space
we stop our ears
lest we should hear tell
of the man in the moon.

13

Summer is
at an end. The migrants
depart. When they return
in spring to the garden,
will there be a man among them?

R. S. THOMAS

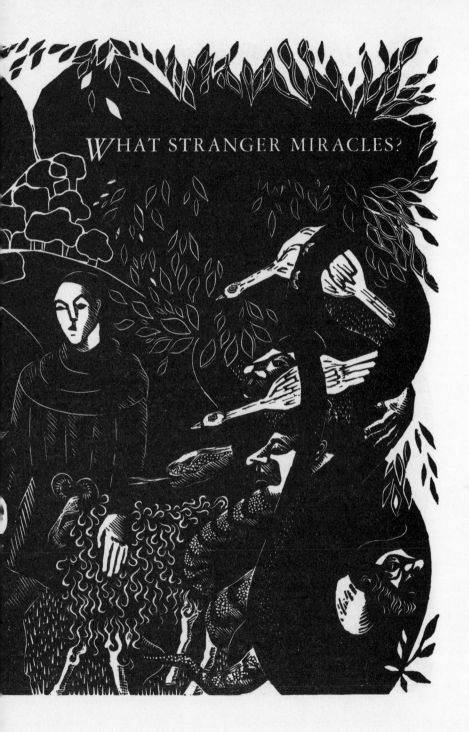

WHAT STRANGER MIRACLES?

If All the World were Paper

If all the world were paper,
    And all the sea were ink,
And all the trees were bread and cheese,
    How should we do for drink?

If all the world were sand-o
    Oh, then what should we lack-o?
If, as they say, there were no clay,
    How should we take tobacco?

If all our vessels ran-a,
    If none but had a crack-a;
If Spanish apes ate all the grapes,
    How should we do for sack-a?

If friars had no bald pates,
    Nor nuns had no dark cloisters;
If all the seas were beans and peas,
    How should we do for oysters?

If there had been no projects,
    Nor none that did great wrongs;
If fiddlers shall turn players all,
    How should we do for songs?

If all things were eternal,
    And nothing their end bringing;
If this should be, then how should we
    Here make an end of singing?

ANONYMOUS

Poetry

What is Poetry? Who knows?
Not a rose, but the scent of the rose;
Not the sky, but the light in the sky;
Not the fly, but the gleam of the fly;
Not the sea, but the sound of the sea;
Not myself, but what makes me
See, hear, and feel something that prose
Cannot: and what it is, who knows?

ELEANOR FARJEON

Hawthorn White

Hawthorn white, hawthorn red
Hanging in the garden at my head
Tell me simple, tell me true
When comes the winter what must I do?

I have a house with chimneys four
I have a silver bell on the door,
A single hearth and a single bed.
    Not enough, the hawthorn said.

I have a lute, I have a lyre
I have a yellow cat by my fire,
A nightingale to my tree is tied.
    That bird looks sick, the hawthorn sighed.

I write on paper pure as milk
I lie on sheets of Shantung silk,
On my green breast no sin has snowed.
 You'll catch your death, the hawthorn crowed.

My purse is packed with a five-pound note
The watchdogs in my garden gloat.
I blow the bagpipe down my side.
 Better blow your safe, the hawthorn cried.

My pulse is steady as my clock
My wits are wise as the weathercock.
Twice a year we are overhauled.
 It's Double Summer-Time! the hawthorn called.

I have a horse with wings for feet
I have chicken each day to eat.
When I was born the church-bells rang.
 Only one at a time, the hawthorn sang.

I have a cellar, I have a spread
The bronze blood runs round my bulkhead.
Why is my heart as light as lead?
 Love is not there, the hawthorn said.

CHARLES CAUSLEY

The Terrible Path

While playing at the woodland's edge
I saw a child one day,
She was standing near a foaming brook
And a sign half-rotted away.

There was something strange about her clothes;
They were from another age,
I might have seen them in a book
Upon a mildewed page.

She looked pale and frightened,
Her voice was thick with dread.
She spoke through lips rimmed with green
And this is what she said:

'I saw a signpost with no name,
I was surprised and had to stare,
It pointed to a broken gate
And a path that led nowhere.

'The path had run to seed and I
Walked as in a dream.
It entered a silent oak wood,
And crossed a silent stream.

'And in a tree a silent bird
Mouthed a silent song.
I wanted to turn back again
But something had gone wrong.

'The path would not let me go;
It had claimed me for its own,
It led me through a dark wood
Where all was overgrown.

'I followed it until the leaves
Had fallen from the trees,
I followed it until the frost
Drugged the autumn's bees.

'I followed it until the spring
Dissolved the winter snow,
And whichever way it turned
I was obliged to go.

'The years passed like shooting stars,
They melted and were gone.
But the path itself seemed endless,
It twisted and went on.

'I followed it and thought aloud,
"I'll be found, wait and see."
Yet in my heart I knew by then
The world had forgotten me.'

Frightened I turned homeward,
But stopped and had to stare.
I too saw that signpost with no name,
And the path that led nowhere.

BRIAN PATTEN

Excelsior

The shades of night were falling fast,
As through an Alpine village passed
A youth, who bore, 'mid snow and ice,
A banner with the strange device,
　　Excelsior!

His brow was sad; his eye beneath
Flashed like a faulchion from its sheath,
And like a silver clarion rung
The accents of that unknown tongue,
　　Excelsior!

In happy homes he saw the light
Of household fires gleam warm and bright;
Above, the spectral glaciers shone,
And from his lips escaped a groan,
　　Excelsior!

'Try not the Pass!' the old man said,
'Dark lowers the tempest overhead,
The roaring torrent is deep and wide!'
And loud that clarion voice replied,
　　Excelsior!

'O stay!' the maiden said, 'and rest
Thy weary head upon this breast!'
A tear stood in his bright blue eye,
But still he answered, with a sigh,
　　Excelsior!

'Beware the pine-tree's withered branch!
Beware the awful avalanche!'
This was the peasant's last goodnight!
A voice replied, far up the height,
    Excelsior!

At break of day, as heavenward
The pious monks of Saint Bernard
Uttered the oft-repeated prayer,
A voice cried through the startled air,
    Excelsior!

A traveller, by the faithful hound,
Half-buried in the snow, was found,
Still grasping in his hand of ice
That banner, with the strange device
    Excelsior!

There, in the twilight cold and grey,
Lifeless, but beautiful, he lay,
And from the sky, serene, and far,
A voice fell, like a falling star,
    Excelsior!

HENRY WADSWORTH LONGFELLOW

The Golden Boy

In March he was buried
    And nobody cried
Buried in the dirt
    Nobody protested
Where grubs and insects
    That nobody knows
With outer-space faces
    That nobody loves
Can make him their feast
    As if nobody cared.

But the Lord's mother
    Full of her love
Found him underground
    And wrapped him with love
As if he were her baby
    Her own born love
She nursed him with miracles
    And starry love
And he began to live
    And to thrive on her love.

He grew night and day
    And his murderers were glad
He grew like a fire
    And his murderers were happy
He grew lithe and tall
    And his murderers were joyful
He toiled in the fields
    And his murderers cared for him
He grew a gold beard
    And his murderers laughed.

With terrible steel
   They slew him in the furrow
With terrible steel
   They beat his bones from him
With terrible steel
   They ground him to powder
They baked him in ovens
   They sliced him on tables
They ate him they ate him
   They ate him they ate him

Thanking the Lord
Thanking the Wheat
Thanking the Bread
For bringing them Life
Today and Tomorrow
Out of the dirt.

TED HUGHES

Unwelcome

We were young, we were merry, we were very very wise,
    And the door stood open at our feast,
When there passed us a woman with the West in her eyes,
    And a man with his back to the East.

O, still grew the hearts that were beating so fast,
    The loudest voice was still.
The jest died away on our lips as they passed,
    And the rays of July struck chill.

The cups of red wine turned pale on the board.
    The white bread black as soot.
The hound forgot the hand of her lord,
    She fell down at his foot.

Low let me lie, where the dead dog lies,
    Ere I sit me down again at a feast,
When there passes a woman with the West in her eyes,
    And a man with his back to the East.

MARY COLERIDGE

The Woman of Water

There once was a woman of water
Refused a Wizard her hand.
So he took the tears of a statue
And the weight from a grain of sand
And he squeezed the sap from a comet
And the height from a cypress tree
And he drained the dark from midnight
And he charmed the brains from a bee
And he soured the mixture with thunder
And he stirred it with ice from hell
And the woman of water drank it down
And she changed into a well.

There once was a woman of water
Who was changed into a well
And the well smiled up at the Wizard
And down down down that old Wizard fell. . .

ADRIAN MITCHELL

88

The Horn

'Oh, hear you a horn, mother, behind the hill?
My body's blood runs bitter and chill.
The seven long years have passed, mother, passed,
And here comes my rider at last, at last
I hear his horse now, and soon I must go.
How dark is the night, mother, cold the winds blow.
How fierce the hurricane over the deep sea!
For a seven years' promise he comes to take me.'

'Stay at home, daughter, stay here and hide.
I will say you have gone, I will tell him you died.
I am lonely without you, your father is old;
Warm is our hearth, daughter, but the world is cold.'
'Oh mother, oh mother, you must not talk so.
In faith I promised, and for faith I must go,
For if that old promise I should not keep,
For seven long years, mother, I would not sleep.

Seven years my blood would run bitter and chill
To hear that sad horn, mother, behind the hill.
My body once frozen by such a shame
Would never be warmed, mother, at your hearth's flame.
But round my true heart shall the arms of the storm
For ever be folded, protecting and warm.'

JAMES REEVES

The Song of Wandering Aengus

I went out to the hazel wood,
Because a fire was in my head,
And cut and peeled a hazel wand,
And hooked a berry to a thread;
And when white moths were on the wing,
And moth-like stars were flickering out,
I dropped the berry in a stream
And caught a little silver trout.

When I had laid it on the floor
I went to blow the fire aflame,
But something rustled on the floor
And someone called me by my name:
It had become a glimmering girl
With apple blossom in her hair
Who called me by my name and ran
And faded through the brightening air.

Though I am old with wandering
Through hollow lands and hilly lands,
I will find out where she has gone,
And kiss her lips and take her hands;
And walk among long dappled grass,
And pluck till time and times are done
The silver apples of the moon,
The golden apples of the sun.

W. B. YEATS

Noah's Ark

It began
When God popped His head
Through the clouds and said:

'Oh you wicked, wicked children
What a mess this place is in
All the violence and corruption
It really is a sin.

I turn my back for five aeons
(For I've other work to do)
Keeping the universe tidy
And I get no thanks from you.

You've grown selfish and conceited
Your manners are a disgrace
You come and go just as you please
You'd think you owned the place.

A telling-off's not good enough
You've grown too big for your flesh
So I think I'll wash my hands of you
And start again afresh.'

He turned full on the tap in the sky
Then picked out the one good man
Pure of heart and strong in arm
To carry out his plan: Noah.

'What I need,' explained God
'Is an arkwright to build an ark, right away.'
Said Noah, 'If I can sir.'
'Of course you can, now get stuck in
I won't take Noah for an answer.'

'I want a boat three storeys high
Aboard which you will bring
Not only your wife and family
But two of every living thing.'

'Even spiders?' asked Noah
(who didn't really like them)
'Even spiders,' said God
(who didn't either).

'Cats and dogs and elephants
Slugs, leopards and lice
Giraffes and armadilloes
Buffaloes, bed bugs and mice.

Antelopes, ants and anteaters
(though keep those last two apart)
Bears from Koala to Grizzly
Horses from Racing to Cart.

Fish will be able to fend for themselves
And besides, a wooden ark
Is not the sort of place to keep
A whale or an angry shark.

And don't forget out feathered friends
For they'll have nowhere to nest.
But vermin will determine
Their own survival best.

Flies, maggots and bluebottles
Mosquitoes and stingers that bite
Will live off the dead and dying
So they'll make out all right.

That seems to be all for now, Noah
The rest is up to you
I'll see you again in forty days
Until then God Bless and Adieu.'

He disappeared in a clap of thunder
(Either that or he banged the door)
And the wind in a rage broke out of its cage
With an earth-splintering roar.

And no sooner was everyone aboard
Than the Ark gave a mighty shudder
And would have been crushed by the onrushing waves
Had Noah not been at the rudder.

Right craftily he steered the craft
As if to the mariner born
Through seas as high as a Cyclop's eye
And cold as the devil's spawn.

And it rained, and it rained
And it rained again
And it rained, and it rained
And it rained, and then . . .
        . . . drip . . .
. . . drop . . .
. . . the last . . .
. . . drip dropped . . .
     . . to a . . .
        . . . stop.

Noah at the helm was overwhelmed
For both cargo and crew were unharmed
Then the wind turned nasty and held its breath
So the Ark became becalmed.

Hither and thither it drifted
Like an aimless piece of jetsam
'Food's running out,' cried Mrs Noah
'We'll perish if we don't get some.'

'Maybe God's gone and forgotten us
We're alone in the world and forsaken
He surely won't miss one little pig
Shall I grill a few rashers of bacon?'

'Naughty, naughty!' said Noah sternly
(For it was the stern that he was stood in)
'I'm ravenous, but bring me a raven
I've an idea and I think it's a good 'un.'

As good as his word, he let loose the bird
'Go spy out for land,' he commanded
But in less than a week, it was back with its beak
Completely (so to speak) empty-handed!

Next he coaxed from its lovenest a dove
'We're depending on you,' he confided
Then gave it to the air like an unwrapped gift
Of white paper, that far away glided.

Then the Ark sat about with its heart in its mouth
With nothing to do but wait
So Mrs Noah organized organized games
To keep animal minds off their fate.

Until one morn when all seemed lost
The dove in the heavens was seen
To the Ark, like an archangel it arrowed
Bearing good tidings of green.

'Praised be the Lord,' cried Noah
(and Mrs Noah cried too)
And all God's creatures gave their thanks
(even spiders, to give them their due).

Then God sent a quartet of rainbows
Radiating one from each side
To the four corners of the earth
Where they journeyed and multiplied.

And as Noah set off down the mountain
To be a simple farmer again
A voice thundered: 'Nice work there sunshine.'
Here endeth the story. Amen.

ROGER McGOUGH

The North Ship

I saw three ships go sailing by,
Over the sea, the lifting sea,
And the wind rose in the morning sky,
And one was rigged for a long journey.

The first ship turned towards the west,
Over the sea, the running sea,
And by the wind was all possessed
And carried to a rich country.

The second turned towards the east,
Over the sea, the quaking sea,
And the wind hunted it like a beast
To anchor in captivity.

The third ship drove towards the north,
Over the sea, the darkening sea,
But no breath of wind came forth,
And the decks shone frostily.

The northern sky rose high and black
Over the proud unfruitful sea,
East and west the ships came back
Happily or unhappily:

But the third went wide and far
Into an unforgiving sea
Under a fire-spilling star,
And it was rigged for a long journey.

PHILIP LARKIN

Mary Celeste

Only the wind sings
in the riggings,
the hull creaks a lullaby;
a sail lifts gently
like a message
pinned to a vacant sky.
The wheel turns
over bare decks,
shirts flap on a line;
only the song of the lapping waves
beats steady time . . .

First mate,
off-duty from
the long dawn watch, begins
a letter to his wife, daydreams
of home.

The Captain's wife is late;
the child did not sleep
and breakfast has passed . . .
She, too, is missing home;
sits down at last to eat,
but can't quite force
the porridge down.
She swallows hard,
slices the top from her egg.

The second mate
is happy.
A four-hour sleep,
full stomach
and a quiet sea
are all he craves.
He has all three.

Shirts washed and hung, beds
made below, decks done, the boy
stitches a torn sail.

The Captain
has a good ear for a tune;
played his child to sleep
on the ship's organ.
Now, music left,
he checks his compass,
lightly tips the wheel,
hopes for a westerly.
Clear sky, a friendly sea,
fair winds for Italy.

The child now sleeps, at last,
head firmly pressed into her pillow
in a deep sea-dream.

Then why are the gulls wheeling
like vultures in the sky?
Why was the child snatched
from her sleep? What drew
The Captain's cry?

Only the wind replies
in the rigging,
and the hull creaks and sighs;
a sail spells out its message
over silent skies.
The wheel still turns
over bare decks,
shirts blow on the line;
the siren-song of lapping waves
still echoes over time.

JUDITH NICHOLLS

The Sands of Dee

'Oh Mary, go and call the cattle home,
And call the cattle home,
And call the cattle home,
Across the sands of Dee!'
The western wind was wild and dank with foam,
And all alone went she.

The western tide crept up along the sand,
And o'er the sand,
And round and round the sand,
As far as eye could see.
The rolling mist came down and hid the land:
And never home came she.

'O is it weed, or fish, or floating hair—
A tress of golden hair,
A drowned maiden's hair,
Above the nets at sea?'
Was never salmon yet that shone so fair
Among the stakes of Dee.

They rowed her in across the rolling foam,
The cruel crawling foam,
The cruel hungry foam,
To her grave beside the sea;
But still the boatmen hear her call the cattle home,
Across the sands of Dee.

CHARLES KINGSLEY

Miracles

Why, who makes much of a miracle?
As to me I know of nothing else but miracles,
Whether I walk the streets of Manhattan,
Or dart my sight over the roofs of houses toward the sky,
Or wade with naked feet along the beach just in the edge of the
    water,
Or stand under trees in the woods,
Or talk by day with anyone I love, or sleep in the bed at night
    with anyone I love,
Or sit at table at dinner with the rest,
Or look at strangers opposite me riding in the car,
Or watch honey-bees busy around the hive of a summer fore-
    noon,
Or animals feeding in the fields,
Or birds, or the wonderfulness of insects in the air,
Or the wonderfulness of the sundown, or the stars shining so
    quiet and bright,
Or the exquisite delicate thin curve of the new moon in spring;
These with the rest, one and all, are to me miracles,
The whole referring, yet each distinct and in its place.

To me every hour of the light and dark is a miracle,
Every cubic inch of space is a miracle,
Every square yard of the surface of the earth is spread with the
    same,
Every foot of the interior swarms with the same.

To me the sea is a continual miracle,
The fishes that swim—the rocks—the motion of the waves—
    the ships with men in them,
What stranger miracles are there?

WALT WHITMAN

WE'LL WEATHER THE WEATHER

Whether

Whether the weather be fine
Or whether the weather be noı
Whether the weather be cold
Or whether the weather be hot—
We'll weather the weather
Whatever the weather
Whether we like it or not!

ANONYMOUS

The Weather

What's the weather on about?
Why is the rain so down on us?
Why does the sun glare at us so?

Why does the hail dance so prettily?
Why is the snow such an overall?
Why is the wind such a tearaway?

Why is the mud so fond of our feet?
Why is the ice so keen to upset us?
Who does the weather think it is?

GAVIN EWART

Weathers

This is the weather the cuckoo likes,
    And so do I;
When showers betumble the chestnut spikes,
    And nestlings fly:
And the little brown nightingale bills his best,
And they sit outside at 'The Travellers' Rest',
And maids come forth sprig-muslin drest,
And citizens dream of the south and west,
    And so do I.

This is the weather the shepherd shuns,
    And so do I;
When beaches drip in browns and duns,
    And thresh, and ply;
And hill-hid tides throb, throe on throe,
And meadow rivulets overflow,
And drops on gate-bars hang in a row,
And rooks in families homeward go,
    And so do I.

THOMAS HARDY

Summer and Winter

It was a bright and cheerful afternoon,
Towards the end of the sunny month of June,
When the north wind congregates in crowds
The floating mountains of the silver clouds
From the horizon—and the stainless sky
Opens beyond them like eternity.
All things rejoiced beneath the sun; the weeds,
The river, and the cornfields, and the reeds;
The willow leaves that glanced in the light breeze,
And the firm foliage of the larger trees.

It was a winter such as when birds die
In the deep forests; and the fishes lie
Stiffened in the translucent ice, which makes
Even the mud and slime of the warm lakes
A wrinkled clod as hard as brick; and when,
Among their children, comfortable men
Gather about great fires, and yet feel cold:
Alas, then, for the homeless beggar old.

PERCY BYSSHE SHELLEY

The Pedalling Man

We put him on the roof and we painted him blue,
And the pedalling man knew what to do—
He just pedalled, yes he pedalled:
He rode through the night with the wind just right
And he rode clear into the morning,
Riding easy, riding breezy, riding
Slow in the sunrise and the wind out of the east.

A weathervane was what he was—
Cast-iron man with a sheet-iron propeller, riding a
Worm gear, holding a little steering wheel,
Iron legs pumping up and down—show him a
Wind and he'd go. Work all day and
All his pay was the weather. Nights, too,
We'd lie in bed and hear him
Creak up there in the dark as he
Swung into the wind and worked up speed,
Humming and thrumming so you could
Feel it all through the house—
The more wind, the faster he went, right through
Spring, summer and fall.

He rode warm winds out of the south,
Wet winds out of the east, and the
Dry west winds, rode them all with a
Serious iron face. Hard-nosed, tight-mouthed
Yankee-looking kind of an iron man.
'Show me a wind and I'll go,' he said.
'I'm a pedalling fool and I'm heading for weather.'
The weather came and he kept on going, right into
Winter, and the wind out of the north had no let up—
We lived on a hill, and wind was what we got a lot of.

Then a night came along, and a blizzard was making,
Windows rattling and the whole house shaking,
But the iron man just hummed with the blast,
Said, 'Come on, wind, and come on fast,
Show me your winter, make it nice and cool,
Show me your weather—I'm a pedalling fool!'
Gears all spinning, joints all shivering,
Sheet-iron clattering, cast-iron quivering till WHOMP!
The humming stopped, and we all sat up in bed with
Nothing to listen to but the wind right through into morning.

And there he was when we dug him out, propeller all bent,
One eye in the snow and one eye
Staring up at the sky, still looking for weather.
He never let on he was beat, not him.

Well, my father put him up on the roof again, this time
Without the propeller.
'Let him ride easy,' he said. 'A man can only take
Just so much north wind, even if he's iron.'

RUSSELL HOBAN

Rain

Beautiful rain
Falling so softly
Such a delicate thing

The harvests need you
And some of the flowers
But we too

Because you remind
Of coolness of quiet
Of tenderest words

Come down rain, fall
Not too harshly but give
Your strange sense of peace to us.

ELIZABETH JENNINGS

The Mud

The glistening mud that loves a gate
Was mashed by cows of late,
But now its puddles lie so still
They hold the clouds and trees and hill;
But when the painted cows come out
From milking-shed to grass
And churn the mud up as they pass,
How cloud and tree and hill will dart about!

ANDREW YOUNG

The Black Cloud

Little flocks of peaceful clouds,
    Lying in your fields so blue,
While my eyes look up they see
    A black Ram coming close to you.

He will scatter you poor flocks,
    He will tear up north and south;
Lightning will come from his eye,
    And fierce thunder from his mouth.

Little flocks of peaceful clouds,
    Soon there'll be a dreadful rout;
That Ram's horns can toss big ships,
    Tear an oak tree's bowels out.

W. H. DAVIES

Storm

They're at it again
the wind and the rain
It all started
when the wind
took the window
by the collar
and shook it
with all its might
Then the rain
butted in
What a din
They'll be at it all night
Serves them right
if they go home in the morning
and the sky won't let them in

ROGER McGOUGH

Thunder and Lightning

Blood punches through every vein
As lightning strips the windowpane.

Under its flashing whip, a white
Village leaps to light.

On tubs of thunder, fists of rain
Slog it out of sight again.

Blood punches the heart with fright
As rain belts the village night.

JAMES KIRKUP

Ice

The North Wind sighed:
And in a trice
What was water
Now is ice.

What sweet rippling
Water was
Now bewitched is
Into glass:

White and brittle
Where is seen
The prisoned milfoil's
Tender green;

Clear and ringing
With sun aglow,
Where the boys sliding
And skating go.

Now furred's each stick
And stalk and blade
With crystals out of
Dewdrops made.

Worms and ants,
Flies, snails and bees
Keep close house guard,
Lest they freeze;

O, with how sad
And solemn an eye
Each fish stares up
Into the sky

In dread lest his
Wide watery home
At night shall solid
Ice become.

WALTER DE LA MARE

Snow in the Suburbs

Every branch big with it,
Bent every twig with it;
Every fork like a white web-foot;
Every street and pavement mute;
Some flakes have lost their way, and grope back upward, when
Meeting those meandering down they turn and descend again.
The palings are glued together like a wall,
And there is no waft of wind with the fleecy fall.

A sparrow enters the tree,
Whereon immediately
A snow-lump thrice his own slight size
Descends on him and showers his head and eyes.
And overturns him,
And near inurns him;
And lights on a nether twig, when its brush
Starts off a volley of other lodging lumps with a rush.

The steps are a blanched slope,
Up which, with feeble hope,
A black cat comes, wide-eyed and thin;
And we take him in.

THOMAS HARDY

Stopping by Woods on a Snowy Evening

Whose woods these are I think I know.
His house is in the village though;
He will not see me stopping here
To watch his woods fill up with snow.

My little horse must think it queer
To stop without a farmhouse near
Between the woods and frozen lake
The darkest evening of the year.

He gives his harness bells a shake
To ask if there is some mistake.
The only other sound's the sweep
Of easy wind and downy flake.

The woods are lovely, dark and deep,
But I have promises to keep,
And miles to go before I sleep,
And miles to go before I sleep.

ROBERT FROST

The Brook

I come from haunts of coot and tern,
  I make a sudden sally,
And sparkle out among the fern,
  To bicker down a valley.

By thirty hills I hurry down,
  Or slip between the ridges,
By twenty thorps, a little town,
  And half a hundred bridges.

Till last by Philip's farm I flow
  To join the brimming river,
For men may come and men may go,
  But I go on for ever.

I chatter over stony ways,
  In little sharps and trebles,
I bubble into eddying bays,
  I babble on the pebbles.

With many a curve my banks I fret
  By many a field and fallow,
And many a fairy foreland set
  With willow-weed and mallow.

I chatter, chatter, as I flow
  To join the brimming river,
For men may come and men may go,
  But I go on for ever.

I wind about, and in and out,
  With here a blossom sailing,
And here and there a lusty trout,
  And here and there a grayling,

And here and there a foamy flake
  Upon me, as I travel
With many a silvery waterbreak
  Above the golden gravel.

And draw them all along, and flow
  To join the brimming river,
For men may come and men may go,
  But I go on for ever.

I steal by lawns and grassy plots,
  I slide by hazel covers;
I move the sweet forget-me-nots
  That grow for happy lovers.

I slip, I slide, I gloom, I glance,
  Among my skimming swallows;
I make the netted sunbeam dance
  Against my sandy shallows.

I murmur under moon and stars
  In brambly wildernesses;
I linger by my shingly bars;
  I loiter round my cresses;

And out again I curve and flow
  To join the brimming river,
For men may come and men may go,
  But I go on for ever.

ALFRED, LORD TENNYSON

Water

Send it cascading over waterfalls,
And break it with a roaring crash across rocks.
Wash in it, cool with it, drink it, heat with it,
Keep fish in it, kill people by the sheer force of it.
Put out fires with it, rust metal with it,
Swim in it, wade in it, dive in it, splash in it, open your eyes in
    it,
Journey across to France on it,
Freeze it and break glass as it expands,
Heat it and put it in radiators to warm the body,
Or just make cement and build with it.
Let it pour from the sky in tiny droplets,
And leave it as dew to make the daffodils sparkle in spring.
Let it flow in rivers, make electricity from it,
Run it along the gutters, washing the stone, and sail boats on it.
Water flowers with it, wash cars with it, make fountains of it,
But most of all
Just leave it shimmering in a river or pool
And watch, but watch carefully or it will go,
And never return.

JONATHAN KINGSMAN

The Hills

Sometimes I think the hills
That loom across the harbour
Lie there like sleeping dragons,
Crouched one above another,
With trees for tufts of fur
Growing all up and down
The ridges and humps of their backs,
And orange cliffs for claws
Dipped in the sea below.
Sometimes a wisp of smoke
Rises out of the hollows,
As if in their dragon sleep
They dreamed of strange old battles.

What if the hills should stir
Some day and stretch themselves,
Shake off the clinging trees
And all the clustered houses?

RACHEL FIELD

Spring Nature Notes

The sun lies mild and still on the yard stones.

The clue is a solitary daffodil – the first.

And the whole air struggling in soft excitements
Like a woman hurrying into her silks.
Birds everywhere zipping and unzipping
Changing their minds, in soft excitements,
Warming their wings and trying their voices.

The trees still spindle bare.

Beyond them, from the warmed blue hills
An exhilaration swirls upward, like a huge fish.

As under a waterfall, in the bustling pool.

Over the whole land
Spring thunders down in brilliant silence.

TED HUGHES

To Daffodils

Fair daffodils, we weep to see
  You haste away so soon;
As yet the early-rising sun
  Has not attained his noon.
     Stay, stay,
    Until the hasting day
     Has run
    But to the evensong;
And having prayed together, we
  Will go with you along.

We have short time to stay, as you,
  We have as short a spring;
As quick a growth to meet decay,
  As you, or anything.
     We die,
    As hours do, and dry
     Away.
    Like to the summer's rain;
Or as the pearls of morning's dew,
  Ne'er to be found again.

ROBERT HERRICK

Joys

We may shut our eyes,
But we cannot help knowing
That skies are clear
And grass is growing;
The breeze comes whispering in our ear,
That dandelions are blossoming near,
That corn has sprouted,
That streams are flowing,
That the river is bluer than the sky,
That the robin is plastering his home hard by.

JAMES RUSSEL LOWELL

Until I Saw the Sea

Until I saw the sea
I did not know
that wind
could wrinkle water so.

I never knew
that sun
could splinter a whole sea of blue.

Nor
did I know before,
a sea breathes in and out
upon a shore.

LILIAN MOORE

The Sea

They wash their hands in it.
The salt turns to soap
In their hands. Wearing it
At their wrists, they make bracelets
Of it; it runs in beads
On their jackets. A child's
Plaything? It has hard whips
That it cracks, and knuckles
To pummel you. It scrubs
And scours; it chews rocks
To sand; its embraces
Leave you without breath. Mostly
It is a stomach, where bones,
Wrecks, continents are digested.

R. S. THOMAS

Old Man Ocean

Old Man Ocean, how do you pound
Smooth glass rough, rough stones round?
  Time and the tide and the wild waves rolling.
  Night and the wind and the long grey dawn.

Old Man Ocean, what do you tell,
What do you sing in the empty shell?
  Fog and the storm and the long bell tolling,
  Bones in the deep and the brave men gone.

RUSSELL HOBAN

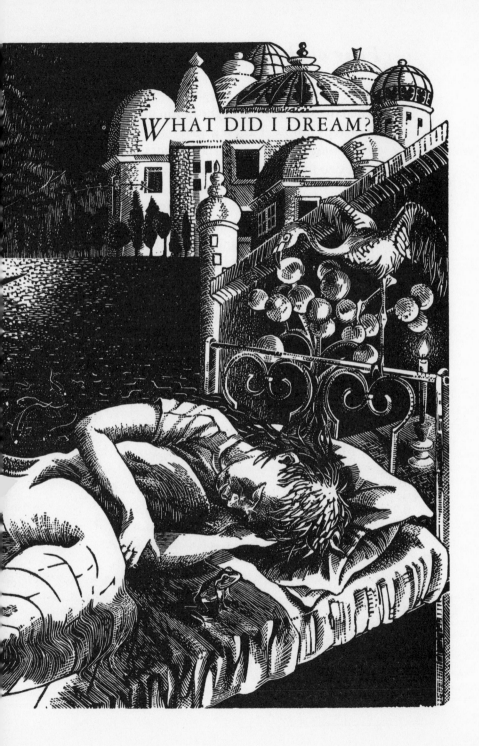

WHAT DID I DREAM?

Fear of the Dark

Along the unlit lane on a night
When the stars are blind, the moon masked,
Footsteps follow. I knew a man
Of six foot three who, on dark nights,
Held two lit cigarettes between his lips
Hoping by this bright stratagem
To fox footpads, mislead murderers.
I used to laugh at him, but not now.
I clench teeth and fists and walk fast.
When I reach the house I switch on lights.
The darkness seems defeated, yet
Open the door, the light does not flow far
Beyond the threshold; it stops dead
A few feet from the step, I hear
The darkness growing; it is enormous.
It is in this room in thin disguise.
I am afraid of it, and with good reason.

VERNON SCANNELL

Night Clouds

The white mares of the moon rush along the sky
Beating their golden hoofs upon the glass Heavens;
The white mares of the moon are all standing on their
hind legs
Pawing at the green porcelain doors of the remote
Heavens!
Fly, mares!
Strain your utmost,
Scatter the milky dust of stars,
Or the tiger sun will leap upon you and destroy you
With one lick of his vermilion tongue.

AMY LOWELL

Is the Moon Tired?

Is the moon tired? She looks so pale
   Within her misty veil;
She scales the sky from east to west,
   And takes no rest.

Before the coming of the night
   The moon shows papery white;
Before the dawning of the day
   She fades away.

CHRISTINA ROSSETTI

Nailsworth Hill

The Moon, that peeped as she came up,
   Is clear on top, with all her light;
She rests her chin on Nailsworth Hill,
   And, where she looks, the World is white.

White with her light – or is it Frost,
   Or is it Snow her eyes have seen;
Or is it Cherry blossom there,
   Where no such trees have ever been?

W. H. DAVIES

Quiet

The night was so quiet
That the hum of the candle burning
Came to my ear,
A sound of breath drawn through a reed
Far off.

The night was so quiet
That the air in the room
Poised, waiting to crack
Like a straining
Stick.

The night was so quiet
That the blood and the flesh,
My visible self sunk in the chair,
Was a power-house giant, pulsing
Through the night.

RICHARD CHURCH

Escape at Bedtime

The lights from the parlour and kitchen shone out
    Through the blinds and the windows and bars;
And high overhead and all moving about,
    There were thousands of millions of stars.
There ne'er were such thousands of leaves on a tree,
    Nor of people in church or the Park,
As the crowds of the stars that looked down upon me,
    And that glittered and winked in the dark.

The Dog, and the Plough, and the Hunter, and all,
    And the star of the sailor, and Mars,
These shone in the sky, and the pail by the wall
    Would be half full of water and stars.
They saw me at last, and they chased me with cries,
    And they soon had me packed into bed;
But the glory kept shining and bright in my eyes,
    And the stars going round in my head.

ROBERT L. STEVENSON

Night Walk

What are you doing away up there
On your great long legs in the lonely air?
    Come down here, where the scents are sweet,
    Swirling around your great, wide feet.

How can you know of the urgent grass
And the whiff of the wind that will whisper and pass
    Or the lure of the dark of the garden hedge
    Or the trail of a cat on the road's black edge?

What are you doing away up there
On your great long legs in the lonely air?
    You miss so much at your great, great height
    When the ground is full of the smells of night.

Hurry then, quickly, and slacken my lead
For the mysteries speak and the messages speed
    With the talking stick and the stone's slow mirth
    That four feet find on the secret earth.

MAX FATCHEN

The Lurkers

On our Estate
When it's getting late
In the middle of the night
They come in flocks
From beneath tower blocks
And crawl towards the light

Down the Crescent
Up the Drive
Late at night
They come alive
Lurking here and lurking there
Sniffing at the midnight air

Up the Shopping Centre
You might just hear their call
Something like a bin-bag
Moving by the wall

Lurking at the bus-stop
Seen through broken glass
Something dark and slimy
Down the underpass

On our Estate
When it's getting late
In the middle of the night
There are things that lurk
About their work
Till dawn puts them to flight.

ADRIAN HENRI

Warning to Children

Children, if you dare to think
Of the greatness, rareness, muchness,
Fewness of this precious only
Endless world in which you say
You live, you think of things like this:
Blocks of slate enclosing dappled
Red and green, enclosing tawny
Yellow nets, enclosing white
And black acres of dominoes,
Where a neat brown paper parcel
Tempts you to untie the string.
In the parcel a small island,
On the island a large tree,
On the tree a husky fruit.
Strip the husk and pare the rind off:
In the kernel you will see
Blocks of slate enclosed by dappled
Red and green, enclosed by tawny
Yellow nets, enclosed by white
And black acres of dominoes,
Where the same brown paper parcel—
Children, leave the string alone!
For who dares undo the parcel
Finds himself at once inside it,
On the island, in the fruit,
Blocks of slate about his head,
Finds himself enclosed by dappled
Green and red, enclosed by yellow
Tawny nets, enclosed by black
And white acres of dominoes,
With the same brown paper parcel
Still unopened on his knee.

And, if he then should dare to think
Of the fewness, muchness, rareness,
Greatness of this endless only
Precious world in which he says
He lives—he then unties the string.

ROBERT GRAVES

Half Asleep

Half asleep
And half awake
I drift like a boat
On an empty lake.
And the sounds in the house
And the street that I hear
Though far away sound very clear.
That's my sister Betty
Playing by the stairs
Shouting like teacher
At her teddy bears.
I can hear Mum chatting
To the woman next door
And the tumble-drier
Vibrates through the floor.
That's Alan Simpson
Playing guitar
While his Dad keeps trying
To start their car.
Dave the mechanic
Who's out on strike
Keeps revving and tuning
His Yamaha bike.

From the open window
Across the street
On the August air
Drifts a reggae beat.
At four o'clock
With a whoop and a shout
The kids from St John's
Come tumbling out.
I can hear their voices
Hear what they say
And I play in my head
All the games that they play.

GARETH OWEN

To Sleep

A flock of sheep that leisurely pass by,
One after one; the sound of rain and bees
Murmuring; the fall of rivers, winds and seas,
Smooth fields, white sheets of water, and pure sky;
I have thought of all by turns, and yet do lie
Sleepless! and soon the small birds' melodies
Must hear, first uttered from my orchard trees;
And the first cuckoo's melancholy cry.
Even thus last night, and two nights more, I lay
And could not win thee, Sleep! by any stealth:
So do not let me wear tonight away:
Without thee what is all the morning's wealth?
Come, blessed barrier between day and day,
Dear mother of fresh thought and joyous health!

WILLIAM WORDSWORTH

Whatif

Last night, while I lay thinking here,
Some Whatifs crawled inside my ear
And pranced and partied all night long
And sang their same old Whatif song:
Whatif I'm dumb in school?
Whatif they've closed the swimming-pool?
Whatif I get beat up?
Whatif there's poison in my cup?
Whatif I start to cry?
Whatif I get sick and die?
Whatif I flunk that test?
Whatif green hair grows on my chest?
Whatif nobody likes me?
Whatif a bolt of lightning strikes me?
Whatif I don't grow taller?
Whatif my head starts getting smaller?
Whatif the fish won't bite?
Whatif the wind tears up my kite?
Whatif they start a war?
Whatif my parents get divorced?
Whatif the bus is late?
Whatif my teeth don't grow in straight?
Whatif I tear my pants?
Whatif I never learn to dance?
Everything seems swell, and then
The night-time Whatifs strike again!

SHEL SILVERSTEIN

Travel

I should like to rise and go
Where the golden apples grow;
Where below another sky
Parrot islands anchored lie,
And, watched by cockatoos and goats,
Lonely Crusoes building boats;
Where in sunshine reaching out
Eastern cities, miles about,
Are with mosque and minaret
Among sandy gardens set,
And the rich goods from near and far
Hang for sale in the bazaar;
Where the Great Wall round China goes,
And on one side the desert blows,
And with bell and voice and drum,
Cities on the other hum;
Where are forests, hot as fire,
Wide as England, tall as a spire;
Where the knotty crocodile
Lies and blinks in the Nile,
And the red flamingo flies
Hunting fish before his eyes;
Where in jungles, near and far,
Man-devouring tigers are,
Lying close and giving ear
Lest the hunt be drawing near,
Or a comer-by be seen
Swinging in a palanquin;
Where among the desert sands
Some deserted city stands,
All its children, sweep and prince,
Grown to manhood ages since,

Not a foot in street or house,
Not a stir of child or mouse,
And when kindly falls the night,
In all the town no spark of light.
There I'll come when I'm a man
With a camel caravan;
Light a flower in the gloom
Of some dusty dining-room;
See the pictures on the walls,
Heroes, fights, and festivals;
And in a corner find the toys
Of the old Egyptian boys.

ROBERT L. STEVENSON

The Unending Sky

I could not sleep for thinking of the sky,
    The unending sky, with all its million suns
Which turn their planets everlastingly
    In nothing, where the fire-haired comet runs.
If I could sail that nothing, I should cross
    Silence and emptiness with dark stars passing;
Then, in the darkness, see a point of gloss
    Burn to a glow, and glare, and keep massing,
And rage into a sun with wandering planets,
    And drop behind; and then, as I proceed,
See his last light upon his last moon's granites
    Die to a dark that would be night indeed:
Night where my soul might sail a million years
In nothing, not even Death, not even tears.

JOHN MASEFIELD

What Did I Dream?

What did I dream? I do not know—
    The fragments fly like chaff.
Yet, strange, my mind was tickled so
    I cannot help but laugh.

Pull the curtains close again,
    Tuck me grandly in;
Must a world of pleasure wane
    Because birds begin

Chattering in a restless tone,
    Rousing me from sleep:
The finest entertainment known,
    And given rag-cheap?

ROBERT GRAVES

Message Understood

The Scantext stutters
'ALERT' in my brain
I await further instructions.
The message comes through.
'SOLUTION CONCERNING THE ROBOTS.'
This has been expected.
I await further instructions.
My personal robot tries to read
The message in my brain
But my hypocrisy defeats him.
He smiles back at my false smile.

In many ways he is almost human.
The message is absorbed.
'THE ROBOTS HAVE OUTLIVED THEIR USE.
THEIR AMBITION THREATENS US.'
I await further instructions.
'LAST WEEK THREE OF THEM
WERE SEEN DANCING AND SINGING
IN THE DESERTED BALLROOM.'
I await further instructions.
'IF EACH HUMAN PLAYS HIS PART
THEN NO ONE WILL BE GUILTY.'
Message understood.
I prime my hand laser.
My robot turns to me
With something in his face
That in a man you might call fear.
For three seconds I squeeze the trigger.
The fine rod of light penetrates him.
He falls to the ground
His eyes turning to water.
Something like a song
Invades his throat
And his mouth leaks red.
Soon the threat will be over
If all humans do their duty.
Humming to myself
I await further instructions.

GARETH OWEN

Moon-Wind

There is no wind on the moon at all
  Yet things get blown about.
In utter utter stillness
  Your candle shivers out.

In utter utter stillness
  A giant marquee
Booms and flounders past you
  Like a swan at sea.

In utter utter stillness
  While you stand in the street
A squall of hens and cabbages
  Knocks you off your feet.

In utter utter stillness
  While you stand agog
A tearing twisting sheet of pond
  Clouts you with a frog.

A camp of caravans suddenly
  Squawks and takes off.
A ferris wheel bounds along the skyline
  Like a somersaulting giraffe.

Roots and foundations, nails and screws,
  Nothing can hold fast,
Nothing can resist the moon's
  Dead-still blast.

TED HUGHES

Ballad of the Sad Astronaut

Why are you weeping, child of the future,
For what are you grieving, son of the earth?
Acorns of autumn and white woods of winter,
Song-thrush of spring in the land of my birth.

You have a new life, child of the future,
Drifting through stars to a land of your own.
With Sirius to guide you, Orion beside you
Wandering the heavens you are free from earth's harm.

I have a new life, the speckled skies' beauty,
Left far behind me the dark cries of earth;
Oh, but I long for the soft rains of April,
Ice-ferned Decembers and suns of the south.

What was I dreaming, to drift with Orion,
To leave for cold Neptune my home and my hearth?
Stars in their millions stretch endless, remind me
Far far behind lies my blue-marbled earth.

Here on the hillside the dawn is just rising,
Buttercups dew-fill, all silken and gold.
Well may you weep, sad child of the future,
Well may you yearn for your beautiful world.

JUDITH NICHOLLS

Our Solar System

We made a model of the Solar System
On our school field after lunch.
Sir chose nine of us
To be planets
And he parked the rest of the class
In the middle of the field
In a thoroughly messy bunch.
'You're the sun,' he brays,
'Big, huge; stick your arms out
In all directions
To show the sun's rays.'
The bit about sticking arms out
Really wasn't very wise
And I don't mind telling you
A few fingers and elbows
Got stuck in a few eyes.
Big Bill took a poke at Tony
And only narrowly missed him,
And altogether it looked
More like a shambles
Than the start of the Solar System.
The nine of us who were planets
Didn't get a lot of fun:
I was Mercury and I stood
Like a Charlie
Nearest of all to the sun,
And all the sun crowd
Blew raspberries and shouted,
'This is the one we'll roast!
We're going to scorch you up, Titch,
You'll be like a black slice of toast!'
Katy was Venus and Val was Earth

And Neville Stephens was Mars,
And the sun kids shouted and
Wanted to know
Could he spare them any of his Bars.
A big gap then to Jupiter (Jayne)
And a bigger one still to Saturn
And Sir's excited and rambling on
About the System's mighty pattern.

'Now, a walloping space to Uranus,' he bawls,
It's quite a bike ride away from the sun.'
Ha blooming ha—at least somebody here's
Having a load of fun.
He's got two planet kids left
And Karen's moaning
About having to walk so far:
She's Neptune—I suppose Sir's
Cracking some joke about
Doing X million miles by car.
Pete's Pluto—'The farthest flung of all,'
Says Sir,
He's put by the hedge and rests,
But soon he starts picking blackberries
And poking at old birds' nests.
'Of course,' yells Sir, 'the scale's not right
But it'll give you
A rough idea.
Now, when I blow my whistle
I want you all to start on your orbits—
Clear?'
Well, it wasn't of course,
And most of the class, well,
Their hearts weren't really in it,
Still, Sir's O.K. so we gave it a go,

With me popping round the sun
About ten times a minute,
And Pluto on the hedge ambling round
Fit to finish his orbit next year.
We'd still have been there but
A kid came out of the school and yelled,
'The bell's gone and the school bus's here!'
Well, the Solar System
Broke up pretty fast,
And my bus money had gone from my sock
And I had to borrow.
I suppose we'll have to draw diagrams
And write about it tomorrow.

ERIC FINNEY

INDEX OF FIRST LINES

A flock of sheep that leisurely pass by 134
A man of words and not of deeds 31
A thumb is half a pinch 34
After the rains 71
Along the unlit lane on a night 126
Anoraks hang limp and folded 8
Armoured dinosaur 71
As he lay dying, two fat crows 47
Asleep he wheezes at his ease 64
Beautiful rain 109
Blood punches through every vein 111
By the lamplight stall I loitered, feasting my eyes 40
Cage bird swung 54
Cats have eyes that yawn 63
Children, if you dare to think 132
Dogs eat gratefully 63
Drake he's in his hammock an' a thousand miles away 44
Every branch big with it 114
Fair daffodils, we weep to see 121
First, in saucers we spread salt 20
Five foot by five foot 17
Flying loose and easy, where does he go 67
Glittering through the sky 72
Go on, I dare you 24
Half asleep 133
Hawthorn white, hawthorn red 79
Here come the hounds alive from the kennels 55
Hey! hey! by this day! 22
How doth the little busy bee 69
I came first through the warm grass 68
I come from haunts of coot and tern 116
I could not sleep for thinking of the sky 137
I kind of exploded inside 4
I'm a lean dog, a keen dog, a wild dog and lone 65
I'm Nobody! Who are you? 30
I quarrelled with my brother 7
I saw three ships go sailing by 96
I should like to rise and go 136
I think I could turn and live with animals, they are 52

I used to like 'Stopping by Woods on a Snowy Evening' 14
I was angry with my friend 32
I went out to the hazel wood 90
If all the world were paper 78
If you wake at midnight, and hear a horse's feet 41
In March he was buried 85
In it there is a space-ship 13
Is the moon tired? She looks so pale 127
It began 91
It is calm 73
It was a bright and cheerful afternoon 106
Johnnie Crack and Flossie Snail 36
Last night, while I lay thinking here 135
'Let's see some super shapes you Blue Group,' 14
Little flocks of peaceful clouds 110
My mind has thunderstorms 33
My name is Tom Bone 48
My Uncle Paul of Pimlico 35
Noah was an Admiral 43
Oh, hear you a horn, mother, behind the hill? 89
Oh Mary, go and call the cattle home 100
Oh! what's the matter? what's the matter? 37
Old Man Ocean, how do you pound 123
On our estate 131
Only the wind sings 97
Poor *Reuben Dixon* has the noisiest school 19
Red is death, for people who are dying 49
See the kitten on the wall 61
She was a dog-rose kind of girl 12
Send it cascading over waterfalls 118
Something told the wild geese 67
Sometimes I think the hills 119
Sticks and stones may break my bones 32
Tails like dandelion clocks 70
The boy had never seen the tree before 26
The boy stood on the burning deck 45
The boy that is good 10
The cat went here and there 58
The flower-fed buffaloes of the spring 66
The glistening mud that loves a gate 109

The lights from the parlour and kitchen shone out   129
The Moon, that peeped as she came up   128
The night was so quiet   128
The North Wind sighed   112
The other side of learning is forgetting   22
The Scantext stutters   138
The shades of night were falling fast   83
The silver swan, who living had no note   66
The sun lies mild and still on the yard stones   120
The teacher has the flowers on her desk   16
The tiger behind the bars of his cage growls   53
The trouble with geraniums   30
The white mares of the moon rush along the sky   127
The wild duck startles like a sudden thought   68
The witches mumble horrid chants   2
There is no wind on the moon at all   140
There once was a woman of water   88
They're at it again   111
They wash their hands in it   123
This is the weather the cuckoo likes   105
Tich Miller wore glasses   11
Today I will not live up to my potential   3
Until I saw the sea   122
You can push   59
You're late, said miss   9
Watch the net drift. Grey tides   57
We made a model of the Solar System   142
We may shut our eyes   122
We put him on the roof and we painted him blue   107
We were young, we were merry, we were very very wise   87
What are you doing away up there   130
What did I dream? I do not know   138
What is poetry? Who knows?   79
What's the weather on about?   104
When chestnuts are hanging   5
Whether the weather be fine   104
While playing at the woodland's edge   81
Whose woods these are I think I know   115
Why are you always tagging on?   6
Why are you weeping, child of the future?   141
Why, who makes much of a miracle?   101

ACKNOWLEDGEMENTS

The editors and publishers are grateful for permission to reproduce the following copyright poems in this anthology:

Marjorie Baldwin: 'The Nature Lesson'. First published in *The Slain Unicorn* (Outposts Publications 1965, ed. Howard Sergeant) and reprinted by permission of the author. **N.M. Bodecker:** 'After the Rain from *Snowman Sniffles*. Reprinted by permission of Faber & Faber Ltd. **Charles Causley:** 'Tom Bone' and 'Hawthorn White' from *Collected Poems* (OUP). Reprinted by permission of David Higham Associates Ltd. **Wendy Cope:** 'Tich Miller', reprinted from *Making Cocoa for Kingsley Amis*, by permission of Faber & Faber Ltd. **John Corben:** 'Glittering through the sky ...'. Used by permission. **W.H. Davies:** 'Thunderstorms', 'The Black Cloud' and 'Nailsworth Hill', reprinted from *The Complete Poems of W.H. Davies* by permission of Jonathan Cape Ltd., on behalf of the Executors of the W.H. Davies Estate. **Olive Dehn:** 'Patterns', reprinted from *The Nine O'Clock Bell* (Viking Kestrel), by permission of the author. **Walter de la Mare:** 'Ice', reprinted from *Collected Rhymes and Verses* (Faber), by permission of The Literary Trustees of Walter de la Mare and The Society of Authors as their representative. **Emily Dickinson: 'I'm Nobody! Who are You?'**. Reprinted by permission of the publishers and The Trustees of Amherst College from *The Poems of Emily Dickinson*, edited by Thomas H. Johnson, Cambridge, Mass.: The Belknap Press of Harvard University Press, Copyright 1951, © 1955, 1979, 1983 by The President and Fellows of Harvard College. **Olive Dove: 'Conversation'.** Reprinted by permission of the author. **Frances Evans: 'Colours'** reprinted from *Round About Eight* (Frederick Warne (Publ.) Ltd.). **Gavin Ewart:** 'The Weather', first published in *Allsorts*, ed. Ann Thwaite (Methuen) and reprinted by permission of the author. **Eleanor Farjeon:** 'The Quarrel' from *Silver Sand and Snow* (Michael Joseph) and **'Poetry'** from *The Children's Bells* (Oxford University Press), both reprinted by permission of David Higham Associates Ltd. **Max Fatchen: 'Night Walk'** and **'Look Out!'**, reprinted from *Songs for My Dog and Other People* (Kestrel Books, 1980), copyright © Max Fatchen, 1980, by permission of Penguin Books Ltd. **Rachel Field: 'Something told the Wild Geese'** and **'The Hills'**, reprinted from *Poems*. Copyright 1934, 1957 by Macmillan Publishing Co., renewed 1962 by Arthur S. Pederson. Reprinted by permission of Macmillan Publishing Company. **Eric Finney: 'Our Solar System'**, first published in *Spaceways* (ed. John Foster, Oxford University Press). Reprinted by permission of the author. **Robert Frost: 'Stopping by Woods on a Snowy Evening'** reprinted from *The Poetry of Robert Frost*, edited by Edward Connery Lathem, by permission of Jonathan Cape Ltd. on behalf of the Estate of Robert Frost. **John Fuller: 'Funeral March'**, reprinted from *Squeaking Crust* (Chatto), by permission of the author. **Wilfrid W. Gibson: 'Sight'**,

reprinted from *Collected Poems 1905–1925*, by permission of Mr M.
Gibson and Macmillan, London & Basingstoke. **Robert Graves: 'Warning to Children'** and **'What did I Dream?'**, reprinted from *Collected
Poems 1975*, by permission of A.P. Watt Ltd., on behalf of The Executors
of the Estate of Robert Graves. **Adrian Henri: 'The Lurkers'** from *The
Phantom Lollipop Lady* (Methuen) (1986). Reprinted by permission of
Rogers, Coleridge and White. **Phoebe Hesketh: 'Sally'**, reprinted from
Song of Sunlight by permission of The Bodley Head. **Russell Hoban:
'The Crow', 'The Pedalling Man'** and **'Old Man Ocean'**, reprinted from
The Pedalling Man, by permission of William Heineman Ltd. **Miroslav
Holub: 'A Boy's Head'**, reprinted from *Selected Poems of Miroslav
Holub*, translated by Ian Milner and George Theiner (Penguin Modern
European Poets, 1967), copyright © Miroslav Holub, 1967, translation
copyright © Penguin Books, 1967, by permission of Penguin Books Ltd.
Jim Howell: 'Cats', 'Dogs' reprinted from *Smoke Signals* by permission
of Peterloo Poets. **Ted Hughes: 'The Golden Boy'** and **'Spring Nature
Notes'** from *Season Songs*; **'Moon Wind'** from *Moon Whales*; **'Roger the
Dog'** from *What is the Truth?*. All reprinted by permission of Faber &
Faber Ltd. **Elizabeth Jennings: 'Rain'**, reprinted from *Lucidities* (Macmillan), by permission of David Higham Associates Ltd. **Brian Jones:
'How to Catch Tiddlers'**, reprinted from *Poems and Family Album*
(London Magazine Editions), by permission of the publisher. **Jonathan
Kingsman: 'Water'**, reprinted by permission of the author. **James
Kirkup: 'Thunder and Lightning'**, first published in *The Prodigal Son*
(OUP) and reprinted by permission of the author. **Philip Larkin: 'The
North Ship Legend'**, reprinted from *The North Ship*, by permission of
Faber & Faber Ltd. **Jean Little: 'Today'** and **'After English Class'**,
reprinted from *Hey World, Here I Am!*, by permission of Oxford University
Press. **Amy Lowell: 'Night Clouds'**, reprinted from *The Complete Poetical
Works of Amy Lowell*, Copyright © 1955 by Houghton Mifflin Company,
Copyright © 1983 renewed by Houghton Mifflin Company, Brinton P.
Roberts, Esquire and G. D'Andelot Belin, Esquire, by permission of
Houghton Mifflin Company. **George MacBeth: 'Fourteen Ways of
Touching the Peter'**, reprinted from *Night of Stones*, by permission of the
author. **Roger McGough: 'Storm'** from *After the Merrymaking* and
'Noah's Ark' from *Waving at Trains*, reprinted by permission of Jonathan
Cape Ltd. **Irene McLeod: 'Lone Dog'**, reprinted from *Songs to Save a Soul*
by permission of the author's estate and Chatto & Windus. **Eric Millward:
'Thumbs'** reprinted from *Appropriate Noises* (Peterloo Poets, 1987), by
permission of the publisher. **Adrian Mitchell: 'The Blackboard'** and **'The
Woman In Water'**, reprinted from *Nothingmas Day*, by permission of
W.H. Allen Publishers. **John Mole: 'Squirrels'** reprinted from *Boo to a
Goose*, by permission of Peterloo Poets. **Lilian Moore: 'Until I Saw the
Sea'**, reprinted from *I Feel the Same Way*, Copyright © 1967 Lilian
Moore, by permission of Atheneum Publishers, an imprint of Macmillan
Publishing Company. **Peter Niblett: 'The Tiger'**, reprinted from *As
Large as Alone* (OUP), by permission of the author. **Judith Nicholls:
'Ballad of the Sad Astronaut'** and **'Late'** from *Magic Mirror*, **'The Dare'**,

149